14 Days

DEC 9 '61
DEC 16 '61
JUL 2 '62
JUL 16 '62
OCT 25 '62

NOV 10 '62
NOV 17 '62
JAN 2 '63

FEB 13 '63

APR 8 '63
APR 17 '63
OCT 11 '63
OCT 12 '64
MAY 12 '66

JUN 15 '66
OCT 4 '66

SEP 27 '67
APR 3 '68
MAY 8 '68

JAN 11 '69
JUL 14 '73
JUL. 16 1985

DEC. 4 1985

W9-BAJ-192

WITHDRAWN

SPIES FOR DEMOCRACY

By Dr. Kurt Singer and Jane Sherrod

Treason has been *Dr. Kurt Singer's* business for twenty-five years.

He was wanted by both the Hitler and the Soviet governments. He has seen revolutions, betrayals, double-crosses and deceptions—and always fought back for the forces of democracy.

As a former intelligence officer, he has written thirty-six books of which the latest is *Spies for Democracy*. This book was co-authored by *Jane Sherrod*, who took the most important and fascinating spy cases from Dr. Singer's books and rewrote them for today's readers.

Spies for Democracy is filled with international intrigue and threads the story of espionage through history—from Biblical days, into America's beginning as a republic, the agents in the Grey and Blue— to the modern space spies.

We meet such American patriots as Nathan Hale, Emma Emmonds, spy during the War Between the States, Mr. J. Edgar Hoover, Herbert J. Philbrick and the first United States space spy to be captured: *Francis G. Powers*. Other chapters tell the story of Sun Yat Sen, Mata Hari's daughter and Commander Crabb, the frogman who spied on Khrushchev. These are only a few characters whose stories are told in this book. This galaxy of spies who have worked for the cause of democracy and freedom make for unforgettable reading.

Dr. Kurt Singer is an internationally known authority on espionage who has addressed countless numbers of students and adults, both in the United States and abroad.

Jane Sherrod (alias Mrs. Kurt Singer) is not only the co-author and co-pilot for this book, but an outstanding educator, former school supervisor, textbook consultant and holds a Master's degree in lan-

(Continued on back flap)

Dedication

To the unsung heroes of education:
the school librarians

SPIES FOR DEMOCRACY

Kurt Singer and Jane Sherrod

Publishers

T. S. DENISON & CO., INC.

Minneapolis

Copyright ©, 1960 by
T. S. DENISON & CO., INC.

All rights reserved, including the right to reproduce this book, or portions thereof, except that permission is hereby granted to reviewers to quote brief passages in a review to be printed in magazines and newspapers.

Printed in the U.S.A.
By THE BRINGS PRESS

International Copyright Secured
Library of Congress Catalog Card Number: 60-14934

920
S

Contents

20129

Introduction

How I Became a Spy:

I was a spy. However, I prefer to call myself an intelligence officer. There is a difference, but it is largely one's point of view. If a person does secret service work for the Russians or the Red Chinese, he is a spy. *But* if he does the same work for Uncle Sam, he rates the title of Intelligence Officer.

It all began a few weeks before the Second World War. I was then stationed in Sweden, the Land of the Midnight Sun, where I worked as a correspondent for a group of American newspapers. It was an interesting, challenging, pleasant life, for the Swedes believe in Democracy as much as we do and, in one respect at least, have been more fortunate than Americans, for they have not been involved in a war for one hundred and fifty years.

One bright day a stranger came to my home and presented to me an absolutely fantastic idea.

"Singer," he said, "I've been watching you for a long time. As a newspaper man you seem to have fine contacts. You speak Swedish, Norwegian and Danish. You speak German, French . . . and some English. Why don't you work for us?"

I was flattered to receive another newspaper assignment, but pressures of work forced me to answer, "I am sorry. I cannot possibly take on another job. I am far too busy now."

My guest looked at me squarely. "I didn't suggest a newspaper assignment at all."

7

I was stunned. What did he have in mind?

"Well," he continued, "it would be a sort of sideline. I want you to keep your eyes and ears open. I want you to meet as many enemy agents as possible and find out what the Germans and the Russians are doing in this part of the world. We will supply you with money, an address in England where you can reach us secretly as often as you pick up any information of value."

This was a wild proposition, and I gave the stranger a wild answer. I showed him the door and raged at him inhospitably, "You had better leave . . . and leave fast. I'll call the police. I have no intentions of becoming involved with spies."

But the man did not leave. He didn't even look frightened. He merely settled firmly in his chair as if he intended to stay for some time. From his briefcase and pockets, he began to pull out papers and documents. I knew I had lost. This gentleman was representing another gentleman: Uncle Sam. I was in!

I don't know what anyone else would have done in my situation, but I knew I possessed less information about spying than the average sixth grader has about rockets to the moon.

In retrospect, the Government had a good reason for selecting me. I served in a voluntary capacity on a refugee committee in Stockholm. Thousands of refugees had fled from their war-torn countries to safety in Sweden. They came from all over Europe, every place Hitler and Stalin had crushed with their heavy heels. These displaced persons arrived from Austria and Czechoslovakia, Poland, Nazi Germany, Estonia, Latvia and Finland. Hidden among them was an untapped wealth of information the Allied governments wanted.

But I knew nothing about the methods of espionage, at least not more than I had seen in movies or read in books. As a youngster I believed spies were the little boys who tried to find out secrets about little girls, and as an adult, my facts of spy operations were still fuzzy, vague and erroneous. I could not go to the United States for training, for I was needed in Sweden. America's entry into the conflict was only a matter of time.

I laugh when I think back about my first day on the job. I went to the nearest library and came home laden with ten books on spies. Publishers do not, I observed, print "How-To-Spy" books.

Next, I saw every motion picture on espionage that was shown in Stockholm, trying to get new ideas. True, I had a marvelous time, but after sitting through half a dozen spy pictures, the stories, the methods, the cloak-and-dagger routines became set formulas dreamed up in the fanciful heads of Hollywood script writers.

The basic screen or television plot is simple.

First, there is a very beautiful woman spy whose charm is exceeded only by her cleverness. She meets a high-ranking enemy officer. He is very handsome. He also has to be a bit on the stupid side, or there would be no movie. Near the end of the first reel, the two fall in love and the second reel depicts the hero's disillusionment when the beautiful blonde with the long cigarette holder steals all the important atomic secrets out of the top drawer of his unlocked desk. From there on, the audience is lead to believe the blonde won the war single-handed, peace comes to all mankind and the fading shot shows the two together in a new country beginning a grand new life together.

Real life is more complicated. It is also less glamorous. There are few beautiful blondes left in the spy game. The plain, mousy girl makes the better spy. No one suspects her, because no one bothers to give her a second glance. Instead of the dashing Scarlet Pimpernel, the gentleman spy of today is half-scientist and half-technician. He does not run around, darting from alley to alley, wearing dark glasses and a false beard. He does not wear a small camera behind his lapel, inside his cuff-link or a radio in his watch. These are old tricks. He does not use invisible ink because any small modern police station can detect such a method of writing within a matter of minutes.

When a spy travels abroad, he does not carry his secret papers in a hidden compartment built into his suitcase because he knows he will have to go through customs and be examined by agents who have fought spies and smugglers for years. Custom officials know every trick in the book. They stop you. They search you. They glance at your shoes. Messages used to be placed between the heel and the sole. These childish methods have been abandoned years ago, but modern technological advancements have created more subtle techniques.

Modern Spy Techniques:

In our scientific age, the secret compartment in a suitcase has been replaced by a microdot. This is a tiny, tiny piece of microfilm no larger than the head of a pin. It is possible to photograph a coded message on the film and glue the microdot on a regular letter. It appears to be a very innocent period *at* the end of a sentence.

In one recent case, the period ended *with* a sentence. A foreigner had lived in the United States for almost eight years. Every day he bought a paper. One afternoon a fourteen-year-old newsboy discovered that a nickel he had been given by someone had split into two parts. There was a strange black dot between the halves. It all lead to the arrest of Colonel Rudolf Ivanovich Abel who was sent to prison for thirty years. But, the rest of the story is in this book.

Of the many other pieces of spy equipment, let me mention one more, a devilish machine adapted from the industrial X-ray. It is portable and when attached to a microphone, a spy can not only take pictures through the walls of an apartment, office, or house, but he can hear what the enemy is plotting as well.

Perhaps the most famous case in the FBI files came when a Soviet spy left the United States with stolen information. Destination: Moscow. When the information reached the FBI offices, the Red agent was half way across the Atlantic.

A special agent phoned Paris for assistance. At the Paris-Orly airport where the plane stopped for refueling, the French police detained the Russian but were unable to find anything suspicious. Next morning when the U. S. agent arrived in Paris from Washington, his first question was, "Did you look into his mouth?"

The French investigators shook their heads.

In a Parisian dentist's office an X-ray was made. There it was! Beneath the gold crown on a molar was a tiny strip of microfilm containing the information of a new and important strategic American patent.

This may sound like a sequence from Dick Tracy, but it happened. The FBI was well informed and intelligent, and, aided by a degree of luck, the Soviet agent was captured.

A spy who is stationed on enemy soil needs to be in touch with his own headquarters. To do this, he often relies upon a short-wave radio. All underground and resistance movements in the last war used this technique. They were guided by strict but justifiable rules. Perhaps the most important of the list of instructions was: *Never repeat yourself.*

Do not broadcast twice from the same place: The enemy can trace your location.

Do not sleep twice in the same locality: The enemy can more easily ambush you.

Travel in groups: Underground parties generally worked in units of three to five people. On the first night they broadcasted from a moving car for never longer than one minute. They then dispersed as rapidly as possible. The second night they sent their messages from the seclusion of a forest, the third, from a field, the fourth, from a fishing boat. A small craft anchored from shore was a favorite for the underground. If the enemy approached, the radio was tossed overboard and the agents looked like casual fishermen. The loss of a radio was quite unimportant when compared with the possible lives saved.

Biblical Spies:

There are nine spy stories in the Bible. Remember when men were sent to Canaan to find out if it really was the land of milk and honey?

And then there was Delilah, the woman spy sent to Samson by the enemy to win his confidence, to gather information, and finally, to break his strength by cutting off his hair.

Women Spies:

In our days women spies know that if they are caught during war time they will be killed just as Mata Hari was. In spite of the great dangers, many brave and intelligent women have and are offering their services to the Intelligence Departments.

Of all the outstanding American women spies in the last war was a lady from Portland, Oregon, whose husband had been killed in combat.

For over three years she spied on shipments in and out of the Philippines during the Pacific campaign and reported to General MacArthur. Risking her life, she smuggled food into the prisons and concentration camps where United States soldiers were starving. Her code name was High Pocket.

Two out of three spies were caught during the last war, and High Pocket was one of them. She was tortured but refused to betray the names of her friends. By a miracle she survived. At the end of the war, High Pocket was decorated by the President of the United States.

The Sitters:

"Sitters" are among the most difficult spies to catch.

It is their job to wait five, ten, twenty years until the right moment to strike.

In this classification, we find the quiet little watchmaker who was planted by the Germans at the harbor of Scapa Flow in Scotland sixteen years before World War II began.

He watched. He waited. He mended watches and made many friends.

But when war came, he was the man who knew the harbor was unprotected. England's great battleship *The Royal Oak* was sunk, taking with her eight hundred thirty-three sailors. You may say *The Royal Oak* was sunk by the torpedo men who sent out the depth charges. You may say it was the captain of the submarine who issued the order. But, if you trace the story back, it was the watchmaker who had waited for sixteen years who gave the information.

The United States was damaged by a "sitter" who brought about the "Day of Infamy," the attack on Pearl Harbor in Honolulu, Hawaii.

Dr. Julius Kuehn and his family arrived on the island of Oahu and told the American Immigration Department a touching refugee story. He received permission to stay in what was not yet our fiftieth state. Dr. Kuehn with the help of his daughter, Ruth, guided the Japanese to the targets of Schofield Barracks and the green-blue harbor where the wealth of the U. S. Pacific fleet lay.

The Double Spies:

May I introduce you to the double spies. They work for two countries at the same time: their own country and the enemy's. This type of secret agent is supposed to give his own country more military information than to the enemy country who is also paying him. The double spy is always mistrusted. He could play the double cross. Intelligence schools tell their new students, "If you know a double spy, or anyone you might suspect to be one, stay away from him. You cannot be sure for whom he really works."

The most famous of all double spies in history was Schulmeister, Napoleon's greatest agent. Living near the Rhine he spoke both German and French which helped him to steal more military information than anyone had ever done before. He was the best spy France ever had. At the same time Austria considered Schulmeister their best spy. But he gave more information to Napoleon than to the Hapsburgs in Vienna. This was one of the many reasons why Napoleon always defeated the Austrian armies.

Shortly before his death, Schulmeister met Emperor Napoleon with a request: "Your Majesty, I have served you long and faithfully. I have one favor to ask. It is not money. But before I die, I wish your Majesty would honor me by granting me one of your medals."

Napoleon's answer has gone down in history. "Schulmeister, I have given you great amounts of money for your services in the past. You may have another half-million francs . . . but I cannot honor a spy!"

After one hundred and fifty years, Napoleon's remark is still true today. There are no honors for the men who spy for money or personal glory. No one likes a traitor: a Benedict Arnold or a Quisling. But honors do exist in the world of espionage. Honors are reserved for the great patriots who were willing to give their lives for their countries as Nathan Hale did, or people like High Pocket, Matt Czwetik, and Herb Philbrick and the hero of the U-2 incident, Francis Powers.

Herb Philbrick is the courageous gentleman who gave nine fantastic years to lead three lives: citizen, counter-spy and communist. Today Philbrick warns us: "there are only one per cent of the entire world's population who are Communists. *But that one per cent controls over one third of the world's territory.*"

Spies on Television:

A spy in a television or movie plot is very different from a real spy. A TV show usually lasts thirty minutes, less the various commercials. In approximately twenty-five minutes, the "agent" is forced to live through an incident that may have taken months, or years, or a lifetime.

If the spy is from an enemy country, the cameras usually show him as short, slightly balding, often dressed in black. He generally speaks with a foreign accent, drinks vodka, and slithers behind doorways.

This mental picture of foreign agents is far from the truth. The most dangerous spies caught in the United States have appeared to be as American as apple pie. Many were reared in good homes and educated in reputable colleges. Some were as fine-mannered and gracious as Alger Hiss.

There is an obvious reason. If the Russian intelligence chief wants an agent to be at Cape Canaveral when the next guided missile is shot, he will not send a spy who speaks with an accent and orders caviar. The Soviet will send someone who is so American he will not be noticed.

For the sake of television drama, a spy must always look like a spy and there must always be a long, suspenseful chase. It makes little difference if the spy is caught sliding down the nose of President Washington at the Mount Rushmore monument in South Dakota, as was depicted in an Alfred Hitchcock thriller, or in the maze of tracks in the New York City subway system. The chase is part of a good spy story. In *The Third Man,* the spy was followed through the sewers of old Vienna. These antics are to tell the audience that the spy is in trouble.

At this point, in most spy stories, the television or film producer plans that the spy will look for a telephone booth. It is always there, and he always has a coin in his pocket. He dials a number. It is never busy. "Hello," he says, "is this Comrade Philbrick (or Smith) . . . I need help."

This is when I turn off the television set, or leave the movie theater. Every spy has strict orders not to phone anyone in a foreign country. The person at the other end may have a tapped phone. It is dubious, too, if any Russian agent would ever say "Comrade" over a telephone in the United States, France, Canada, or any free country.

For the sake of drama and suspense, both television and motion pictures get away with murder—and there are plenty of both on the screen. Meanwhile, in real life, those who are the true spy bosses can get away with murder in espionage too.

The Untouchables:

The "Untouchables" in the spy game are the intelligence chiefs. They are so high in their government positions they cannot be touched.

How do they operate?

Here is a classic example: A Soviet spy defected. By that is meant he decided to switch sides. At the risk of his life,

Mr. X escaped to West Berlin and was flown to Washington. There he told the FBI everything he knew.

Mr. X met Mr. J. Edgar Hoover, the FBI director, and stated the Russians had stolen some very important documents. These papers, said Mr. X, had been copied inside the foreign registration office in Washington. Experts felt a woman had written the copies.

Mr. Hoover began an investigation. After narrowing down the facts, there could be only one woman who had access to the material. Her name was Judy Coplon.

She was watched, followed, shadowed and guarded for three months. The FBI agents could find only that she was loyal, hardworking and apparently guiltless. They lost interest and recommended that the case be dropped.

But Mr. Hoover possesses some qualities of a bulldog. Added to his keen sense of patriotism, he is a man who never stops until a case is cleared and clean.

He planted a trap. An important sounding letter was placed on Miss Coplon's desk.

Ten days later Judy left Washington, leaving notice she was seeing her sick mother in Brooklyn and would not return for a few days.

Eight men were waiting and watching in New York when her train arrived.

Judy did not take a subway to Brooklyn, nor did she make a call to her ailing mother. Instead she went up Broadway and met a man to whom she delivered papers.

Miss Coplon was captured, but her diplomatic spy boss could not be arrested by the FBI.

Spy bosses are government officials with "diplomatic immunity." They cannot be arrested for fear of retaliations.

All the U. S. government could do, in the Coplon and similar cases, was to deport the official. A diplomatic passport is the best secret weapon a spy carries. It also insures him of carrying a diplomatic pouch which is locked and never undergoes inspection at customs. The United States has now installed Geiger counters at entry and departure stations so we can, at least, check to find if atomic material is about to be transported.

A Personal Word:

All these things have been my business for over twenty years. I have gone through wars, revolutions, watched the helpless die and the guilty be punished. When asked, I choose to tell little or nothing of my own experiences. Some are still classified and others too difficult to recount.

Try to put yourself in my position. Imagine you are watching an enemy battleship crawl into a Norwegian harbor. The craft is badly damaged. The water front city is commanded by Hitler's soldiers and Quisling's storm troopers. In the hills, five members of the Norwegian underground watch day after day, getting information from delivery boys, wharf workers, clerks . . . anyone who has a piece of fact or bit of rumor.

Two months later the ship leaves during a frigid Arctic morning at three o'clock and is swallowed in the blackness.

The underground knows the battleship is pulling out of the harbor. They shortwave the message to Allied headquarters in England.

Seven hours later the pride of the Nazi Navy lay at the bottom of the ocean. Two thousand enemy sailors were dead. The press called it a victory. Textbooks refer to the event today.

But the two thousand sailors were two thousand sons of two thousand mothers. No spy or intelligence officer ever wants to tell these mothers he was instrumental in killing their sons.

For this reason, important spy stories are never told in the first person. This book tells of spies and saboteurs, kidnappers, traitors, fakers, deceivers and heroes. If the stories are told in the third person, it is because it is easier that way . . . and safer for everyone.

This book represents the best of my spy stories written over a period of twenty-five years. It includes a few chapters where spies try to destroy democracy. But these few chapters were not eliminated, because they showed how counterspies finally triumphed over deception, betrayal and the grave diggers of democracy.

Jane Sherrod, my wife and co-pilot, has taken these true spy stories, edited and re-written them for the young generation.

KURT SINGER
Buena Park, California

CHAPTER ONE

The Quakeress Who Saved*
George Washington's Army

While the British occupied Philadelphia during the Revolutionary War, most of their time was given to the pleasures of life. It was this fact that caused Franklin to say that Howe had not taken Philadelphia but Philadelphia had taken Howe. There was, however, one serious attempt made to destroy Washington's army during the period and, curiously enough, it was frustrated by the courage, the wit, and the promptness of a brave Quakeress.

When the British took over the city, the officers moved into the most desirable dwellings and set up their headquarters. General Harris confiscated the home of General Cadwalader, on Second Street, four doors below Spruce. Opposite this, on the corner of Little Dock Street, was the quaint home of William and Lydia Darrah, members of the Society of Friends, whose members oppose war in any form.

The Adjutant-General of the British army decided to make his home with the Darrahs. Both pretended to be delighted with the arrangement. The Englishman found a desirable and well-kept colonial house for his temporary home,

---

*From 3000 Years of Espionage.

21

and the Darrahs soon discovered their war guest was a gentleman.

Lydia Darrah was a Whig, and she gloried in it. She made no secret of her feelings to her lodger. One day when he scolded her for being disloyal to England, she exclaimed with spirit:

"I hope thee is beaten. Thee deserve to be for coming across the ocean to conquer a liberty-loving people."

He laughed at this outburst and remarked:

"I was beginning to flatter myself that you and your husband looked upon me as a friend."

"And so we do. We oppose the sin while pitying the sinner. Though we consider thee as a public enemy, we regard thee as a private friend. While we detest the cause thee fights for, we wish well to thy personal interest and safety."

"Oh!" he cried, jovially. "That sounds better. You are really a friend of the King."

"Thee must not feel flattered," she said gravely. "We are for the Colonists. Thee knows that every unnecessary expense has been cut down in this house. Tea has not been drunk since last Christmas. Nor have I bought a new cap or gown since your defeat at Lexington. Be assured that such is the feeling of American women."

The Adjutant-General admired the spirit of such a woman. She was not deceitful. She did not attempt to find favor with the British. It rather pleased him to let her say treasonable things. There certainly could be no danger from this sweet-faced little woman with the poke bonnet and the drab dress. There was no bitterness in her tone or manner.

The Adjutant-General had arranged for a room on the first floor to be used as a sort of conference chamber for the British officers. Here groups of the leading redcoats often assembled by candlelight, for the purpose of discussing plans of campaigns. Several of these gatherings had been held without attracting any particular attention from Lydia Darrah.

Early in December, 1777, there was a strange halt in the round of pleasure among the British officers in Philadelphia. The men were drilled and organized as if in anticipation of a coming movement. There was much new activity. Lydia, who was a true patriot, watched anxiously. She suspected bad days ahead.

On the 2nd of December the Adjutant-General sent for her. She noticed that he was very serious.

"I wish to tell you," he said, "that we will need the use of the sitting room at seven o'clock this evening. We may remain late, and it is important that we should not be disturbed. For this reason I ask you to have all members of your family go to bed early. When we are through and it is time for us to leave I will call you so that you may let us out. Do you understand?"

"Perfectly," she replied. "I will see that everything is prepared. We shall retire and wait until thee summons me."

That night she carried out all of his orders. But she could not rest. The words of the British officer had filled her with curiosity and uneasiness. What did it mean? What was the object of this mysterious conference? Finally she could remain in her room no longer. She crept silently downstairs and stood outside the door where the officers were assembled. By pressing her ear close to the crack she could hear the talk inside the room. The words "Washington" and "Whitemarsh" attracted her attention. Presently she pieced together their plans.

She was shocked. She had heard an order for all the British troops to march out on the evening of the fourth to attack the army of General Washington camped at Whitemarsh. She knew what that would mean. Surprised by a larger army, the patriots would be destroyed. And that destruction meant that the torch of liberty would be extinguished. The hope of freedom would be destroyed.

Lydia Darrah crept silently upstairs again and went to bed, but not to sleep. She was depressed and disheartened. While the members of her family slept, and the officers in the room below perfected their plans, she wondered what could be done to save the American army.

While her mind searched for a solution, there came a rap at her door. The Adjutant-General said they were ready to leave. She remained perfectly quiet. He knocked a second time, louder than before. Still no answer. He pounded with his fists. She arose, taking her time to dress, appeared at the door, candle in hand, and pretended to be very drowsy. He apologized for waking her and left the house with his companions.

Lydia was so excited she could neither sleep nor eat. The question was how to get the information to General Washington. She did not talk to anyone—not even her husband. She decided to go to Whitemarsh herself. She told her family she needed a sack of flour from the mill at Frankford.

"Send one of the servants," her husband said. "There is no good reason why thee should make such a long trip."

"No," she replied. "I shall go myself."

"But at least," he pleaded, "take one of the servant maids with thee."

"I shall go alone," she insisted. She was so stubborn he had to agree.

William Darrah learned on that occasion that even a gentle Quakeress can be quite as obstinate as other members of her sex. He gazed wonderingly at the poke-bonneted woman as she left the house and started in the direction of General Howe's headquarters to get her pass to cross the British lines.

General Howe received her kindly. He knew that the Adjutant-General of his army was quartered at the Darrah home and he thought Lydia was an interesting but harmless rebel. He gave her the pass.

"Don't stay long," he smiled. "Your British guests will miss you."

Lydia hurried away. Once out of sight of the general's headquarters, she ran until she reached Frankford. She left her bag at the mill and continued her journey to Whitemarsh.

Washington was reinforced by 1200 Rhode Island troops and nearly 1000 Virginia, Maryland, and Pennsylvania soldiers. He was now within fourteen miles of Philadelphia. By a resolution of Congress all persons taken within thirty miles of any place occupied by the British troops, in the act of conveying supplies to them, were subjected to martial law. Acting under the resolution, Washington detached large bodies of militia to scour the roads above the city, and between the Schuylkill and Chester, to intercept all supplies going to the enemy.

This served a double purpose. It harassed Howe by preventing him from receiving the supplies, and it gave them to the Continentals. All this time Washington was observing a prudent policy. He was anxious to fight, but he was only willing to do so under circumstances that would be advantageous to himself. He had many critics of this policy, and some of them said nasty things, but Washington held steadily to his purpose in spite of good and evil reports.

Lydia Darrah plodded along to Whitemarsh, not noticing the icy weather or her wet, soggy clothing. Her one thought was to warn Washington.

When she had almost reached her destination, she began to feel footsore and weary. She felt a great desire to sit by the roadside and rest, but she kept on. Beneath those modest and peaceful garments there was a grim determination that ignored suffering.

Just before she reached her goal she saw a mounted Continental officer. His back was turned to her and she wondered if she should speak to him. Before she reached a conclusion, he had twisted about in his saddle and looked in her direction. Both were surprised for they knew each other. He was Lieutenant Colonel Craig, a young American officer. He was amazed to see her, and rode over.

"Have you lost your way?" he asked. Before she could answer he added, "And how did you get through the British lines?"

"I came to get flour at the mill in Frankford. General Howe was good enough to give me a pass."

"But you are beyond Frankford," he protested.

"Perhaps," she answered, "I may be in search of my son who is an officer in the American army."

"Perhaps," retorted Lieutenant Colonel Craig, doubtfully.

By this time several soldiers approached. Lydia became nervous and ill at ease. She plucked at his coat.

"Dismount and walk aside with me," she whispered. "I have something to tell you."

He did as she asked. Little did he suspect that such important news was at hand. They walked some yards from the soldiers.

"Now," he commanded, "tell me what you are doing so far from home."

"Colonel," she cried in a voice that trembled in spite of herself, "I came to warn General Washington that General Howe intends to attack the Continental army. He hopes to find General Washington unprepared."

"How do you know this?"

"I overheard it last night. The Adjutant-General and other officers met at my house to make their plans. I felt that General Washington must be warned, and I walked here for that purpose."

The eyes of the young officer almost started out of their sockets. He gazed down at the frail woman in amazement and admiration.

"Shall I take you to the General?"

"No, it is enough for you to know. It shall be your duty to tell him. And you must agree not to tell your source of information. If it were known that I came here, it would go hard with me. It might mean my death."

"I promise!" he said, solemnly.

The Quakeress told him all that had taken place in her house at the conference among the British officers. She had an excellent memory and was able to give him all the details of the proposed attack. As she concluded she said:

"You must not reveal my identity—even to your men."

"It shall be as you wish, and now you must have rest and food."

She protested feebly, but he insisted upon escorting her to a nearby farmhouse where she might eat and rest before taking the long walk back to the city. She urged him to go to Washington at once. The message he had was more important than her personal comfort. But the lieutenant was a gentleman as well as a patriot. He refused to leave her until she was fed and comfortable. On leaving he stooped and kissed her hand.

"You have saved the army," he said. "You will not be forgotten as long as liberty endures."

Lydia did not stay long and, after a light meal, left for Philadelphia. She paused at Frankford to get the sack of flour, which she carried with her as a proof of the statement that she had gone to the mill. She reached her home safely, and the incident was forgotten by the other members of the household.

But she could not be calm until she was sure the Continental army was safe. She waited eagerly for the departure of the British. Forty-eight hours after her return from Whitemarsh, the beating of drums and the tramping of many feet announced the departure of the British troops. Lydia Darrah stood on the sidewalk as the cavalcades passed by. Apparently she was only a spectator, but actually Lydia was the heroine of the drama. After the last of the soldiers had departed, she went to her room to pray for Washington and his army.

General Howe was in high good spirits. He felt that he was going to catch the "old fox" sleeping. The thought made him chuckle with delight. The town was full of British sympathizers, too, and many of them would have been pleased if the "rebels" received a crushing blow. But Lydia Darrah, in her darkened chamber, hoped that all might go well with Washington and his men.

In the meantime, at Whitemarsh, preparations to meet the British were going on. Washington was impressed with the information Lieutenant Colonel Craig brought him. On the 4th the Commander-in-Chief received word which confirmed the warning carried to the camp by Lydia Darrah. He planned his counter attack and sent McLane, with 100 men, to reconnoiter. This gallant officer met the enemy at eleven o'clock at night on the Germantown road, attacked it, and forced it to change its line of march.

It was three o'clock in the morning before the alarm gun announced the approach of the main body of the British army. They appeared at daybreak and took their position at Chestnut Hill within three miles of Washington's right wing. Here the redcoats met a second surprise. A detachment of the Pennsylvania State Militia gave battle to the enemy. It was a draw, with a few dead and wounded on each side. The British general in charge exclaimed:

"They don't seem to be a bit surprised!"

General Howe passed the day planning and at night changed his ground and moved to a hill on the left within a mile of the American line. He wanted to get into action, but Washington held back his fire. There were several sharp skirmishes at Edge Hill, but no general engagement.

On the morning of the seventh it looked as if Howe intended to attack on the left wing. This was what Washington wanted. His hopes ran high as he prepared for action. In the course of the day he rode through every brigade, explaining how the attack was to be met and urging the men to remember they were fighting in the cause of liberty. Both his words and his manner impressed them, for Washington was grave and determined, which filled his followers with confidence.

The day wore on with nothing but minor skirmishes. An attack was next expected during the night, but it never occurred. The spirit displayed by the Americans, and especially their preparedness, had discouraged the British.

When the first gray tints of dawn appeared the British army was in motion again. But they did not advance toward the Americans. On the contrary, they filed off to the right where long strings of fires were lit. Behind these fires the redcoats silently departed toward Philadelphia.

They had come on a fool's errand. Like the king's soldiers in the rhyme, they had marched up the hill and then marched down again.

Washington immediately sent small firing parties to fall upon the rear of the departing army, but they had made too long a start to be very seriously damaged. The Continentals did, however, succeed in making the redcoats regret they had left Philadelphia.

Washington was sorry there had not been a battle. He wrote to the President of Congress:

"I sincerely wish they had made an attack. At the same time I must add, that reason, prudence and every principle of policy forbade us quitting our post to attack them. Nothing but success would have justified the measure, and this could not have been expected from their position."

It was a sorry procession of Englishmen that filed through the streets of Philadelphia after this historic retreat. They had gone out with high hopes; they returned unsuccessful. They had expected to throw themselves upon a camp of sleeping and unprepared men. Instead they found a spirited and fully prepared foe. The Tory ladies who lined the sidewalks of the city felt sorry for the nonconquering heroes. But one woman watched that mournful march with pleasure, the woman who was chiefly responsible for it—Lydia Darrah.

On the night after the return of the British troops the Adjutant-General of the army sent for Lydia Darrah. He asked her to come to his room as he wished to ask her some important questions. She followed, quaking in her shoes. She felt that someone had betrayed her, and she prepared to suffer the consequences.

"What I wish to know," he said, after she had been seated, "is whether any of your family was up after eight o'clock on the night that I met with the other officers in your sitting room?"

She shook her poke-bonneted head.

"Thee knows that we all went to bed at eight o'clock," she answered.

"I know that you were asleep," he said, "because I had

to knock at your chamber door three times before you awakened. But I wondered if anyone else was about."

"Why?"

"Because someone must have given Washington information. I know you were in bed. You say the others were also. I can't imagine who gave us away unless the walls had ears. When we reached Whitemarsh we found all their cannon mounted and the soldiers ready for us. Consequently, after wasting days in marching, we were forced to come back here like a pack of fools."

"I sympathize with thee," she said, but if one could have peeped beneath the folds of that poke bonnet one would have seen a twinkle in her eyes and a smile of satisfaction on her face.

And who will have the heart to find fault with the brave Quakeress for the twinkle, the smile, and the white lie?

CHAPTER TWO

Nurse and Spy of the Civil War

Although any number of women were spies for the North and the South through the Civil War, Emma Edmonds was in a class alone.

This woman actually lived the stories of which she later wrote. Eleven times she penetrated the Confederate lines. She was a capable person who could not be discouraged. She put on the disguise of a colored servant or spoke the language of an Irish woman peddling cakes from her wicker basket. Dressed as a gawky country lad, she clerked in a Louisville store and picked up information at the same time. In an emergency, she wore military uniforms and became an aide-de-camp.

All this is astounding because Emma Edmonds trained to become a nurse with ambitions of serving as a medical missionary. But the times changed her plans. She found herself, like a tennis ball played by Fortune, batted across the net set by the war between the states. Finally her health broke, and she was given an honorable discharge.

Emma Edmonds was a Canadian, born and educated in

the Province of New Brunswick. From her serious and solemn Presbyterian parents she inherited a hearty strain of religion. She believed in the Bible and in doing good for her fellow men. She dreamed of an assignment to some tropic Borrioboolagha, "on the left bank of the Niger."

The family moved to the States and settled in New England. Emma Edmonds was in New York City on April 12, 1861, that day when the aged Edwin Ruffin fired the first gun of the Civil War.

Emma knew war meant wounded fighting men; and wounded fighting men deserved the best of care. She abandoned her homeward journey and dreams of darkest Africa to volunteer as a nurse in the forces of the North.

She had spent five years in the states when Fort Sumter fell. But in those years she had been convinced the Negro slaves should be freed. Her religious convictions gave her a puritanical intolerance against anything connected with slavery. Two days after the fall of Fort Sumter, Lincoln issued his call for 75,000 men.

Ten days later, Emma was on her way to Washington.

She was not assigned hospital duties or a soft appointment at an executive's desk. She was to wait for the first battle and hurry to the scene of action. Once there, she was to remain as a field nurse.

Two months passed. The North and the South marked time. Each called for more men and moved about seeking good positions for the coming fight. Washington was crammed with invalids. Untrained troops gave way to pure exhaustion. Improper food, impure water and unsanitary drainage brought dysentery and typhoid.

On July 21 came the Battle of Bull Run. Emma was one of the gay crowd that left Washington to make a holiday of that first battle. But unlike the mob that fled before the downfall in confusion, she remained in the field to minister to the dead and the dying. Under fire she proved herself tireless and courageous. She divided her time between her duties and hiding from the enemy as she made her way to Centerville.

When the Confederates overran the village, she climbed a backyard fence and set off across the fields. It was night and a heavy rain beat down upon her. She reached Alexandria at noon the next day. Her shoes were worn to shreds. Her feet were so sore she could hardly walk. But two days later she was back in Washington.

This was Emma Edmond's fiery baptism in the Civil War.

Washington was at its lowest point. Pennsylvania Avenue was a rutted roadway that turned liquid mud with the rain. The streets were filled with senators and federal folk, society matrons and Negro washerwomen, the rich and the poor, gamblers, swindlers and looters. Men who had lost their regiments tried to find them again.

With the fall of Fort Sumter, government investigators were ordered south. Others, covering the formation of the Confederate government, served in an unofficial capacity. Their identities and missions were concealed.

It was while Emma Edmonds was with McClellan's forces in the vicinity of Yorktown that the call came. She changed from a nurse to a spy. A detachment of the Thirty-seventh New York regiment, returning with prisoners from an expedition, brought information that a Federal spy was to be shot in Richmond. The camp chaplain suggested the nurse as a replacement. Few women spies operated through the lines and while danger was still there, their opportunities were far broader than those of the men. Word was passed, and McClellan sent for her.

What were her views on the rebellion? She hated slavery.

Why did she wish to volunteer for so dangerous an undertaking? To serve her adopted country.

What did she know of horses and firearms? She was a skillful horsewoman and an expert with a pistol.

They did not give her a course in espionage. Instead, a phrenologist felt the bumps on her skull and said she was resourceful, capable and trustworthy. Emma was given the oath of allegiance—for the third time—and embarked upon her career as a spy.

Emma Edmonds had a slight figure, almost like a boy's. A steel engraving shows her in the riding habit of the period. Her face was square and determined; her nose somewhat flat, her long hair in unkempt locks, and her black eyes piercingly brilliant. Yet it stretches the imagination to picture her posing as a colored slave—and a male one at that—crossing the lines into enemy territory.

At Fort Monroe, she picked up the clothing of a Negro fieldhand. Her head was shaved by the company barber, and from Washington she obtained a wig of real Negro hair.

"Head, face, neck, hands and arms were colored black as any African," she wrote in her diary. One wonders how the prim little woman managed her disguise. She was to go into the enemy's camp as a male Negro. She was to live as a black man, not only as one of his race, but of his sex as well. What make-up could be applied that would last through days and nights, withstand washing, wind and rain, yet not fade to betray her secret?

We can only conclude Emma exaggerated a bit while writing her own story. It is likely she colored her skin with repeated applications of walnut juice until she assumed the golden brown of a mulatto.

To make certain her disguise was perfect, she returned to camp and hired out as a handyman to the company physician under whom she served. Neither he, the chaplain who recommended her, nor his good wife, recognized that their colored servant was Emma, the nurse.

Convinced that all was well, Emma Edmonds set forth on her first great adventure.

Her destination was Yorktown, her mission to report on troops, conditions, fortifications, and the enemy's plans. With a few hard crackers in her pocket and a loaded gun, Emma Edmonds slipped through the Union lines. It was a dark night. By midnight she had passed the Confederate pickets. Without blanket or covering, she lay on the ground to rest.

A squad of contrabands with rations for the outpost guard awakened her at daybreak. She begged a slice of corn bread and hot coffee. When they marched back into Yorktown she was in their midst. The Negroes returned to their work on the fortifications. Emma found herself confronted by an officer.

"Who's your master?" he saked.

"I dusn't belong to nobody, Massa. I's free and allus was. I's gwine to Richmond to work."

"Take that black rascal and set him to work," a civilian overseer interrupted. "If he doesn't work well, tie him up and give him twenty lashes, just to impress him that there's no free niggers here while there's a damned Yankee left in Virginia."

Pickaxe, shovel, and a heavy wheelbarrow were given her. All day she pushed her loads up a narrow plank to the top of an eight-foot platform. Her muscles ached, her legs lagged, and by nightfall, her hands were a mass of blisters. Painfully she drew a sketch of the outer works and listed the armament:

"Fifteen three-inch rifled cannon; eighteen four and one-half inch rifled cannon; twenty-nine thirty-two pounders; twenty-one forty-two pounders; twenty-three eight-inch Columbiads; eleven nine-inch Dahlgrens; thirteen ten-inch Columbiads; fourteen ten-inch mortars; and seven eight-inch siege howitzers.

She hid her notes in the inner sole of her workshoe, turned in and slept the dead sleep that comes from hard labor.

It was on the second day that suspicion first pointed to her. She had traded places with a waterboy by giving him five dollars. Lee had come to say Yorktown could not long stand the brunt of McClellan's guns. General J. E. Johnston arrived with more soldiers to bring the neighboring forces to 150,000.

Emma looked and listened while she carried her water-pail to the laboring workmen. One of them eyed her above the dripping dipper.

"Jim," he said, "I'll be darned if that feller ain't turnin' white. If he ain't, then I'm no nigger."

"I 'spected to 'come white," Emma promptly replied. "My mudder's a white woman."

Amid their laughter she beat a hurried retreat. A small pocket glass proved the truth. Her make-up was slowly fading and in some places was nearly white. She retouched the telltale spots with a weak solution of nitrate of silver, and decided to leave at the first opportunity.

That afternoon she spotted a peddler from the Federal camp as a spy bringing details of McClellan's outfit. The day passed slowly as did the next. In the evening she was detailed to carry food to an outer post. Soon after she was assigned as a temporary replacement for a guard killed by a sharpshooter. With darkness came the rain. She fled toward the Federal lines, hiding in a ditch until daybreak when she returned to make her report.

The Confederate rifle that she brought with her is now in a federal museum in Washington.

It was no small task to bleach her darkened skin, and her hands were so tender the slightest touch brought stinging pain. But Emma Edmonds removed what make-up she could and returned to her nursing. She watched the evacuation of Yorktown and followed the troops to Williamsburg and Fort Magruder. And while McClellan moved two corps within six miles of Richmond, she heard, for the first time, a thousand voices joined in a rousing chorus:

"Mine eyes have seen the glory of the coming of the Lord."

Julia Ward Howe, a dabbler in literature, had penned the verses one restless night by flickering candlelight beside her child's crib. Little did she know the song would be long remembered when her other works were forgotten.

With time came orders for Emma's second expedition

across the lines. Obviously it was tempting Fate to use again
the same disguise. A female Irish peddler fitted the occasion
better. Numbers of these camp followers were selling their
wares to the soldiers. These Little Buttercups were accepted
without question and never given a second glance.

It was not difficult to procure a dress and basket for her
purpose. Pies, cakes, and knicknacks could be obtained anywhere. After a few days devoted to perfecting the brogue of
the "rale ould stock of bogtrotters," the nurse slipped away,
as perfect in her part as a character from a Boucicault melo-
drama.

This time she went by water. The bridges across the
Chickahominy were not finished so she packed her disguise
with her pies and notions, mounted her faithful horse Frank,
and swam the river. On the opposite shore, she headed her
mount homeward and watched him scramble up the other
bank where a soldier awaited him.

Night clamped down. She had no knowledge of the Confederate picket lines. To press forward was to invite death
from some outpost. She was in the Chickahominy Swamp
with all its mysterious night life threatening her on every
side. Though she had strapped her basket to her back, it
was soaked through. Her foodstuffs were ruined, her notions
sadly damaged. A hospital quilt was sopping as was her
peddler's costume.

Scarcely had she reached the other side of the river
than she realized she was ill—terribly ill. Burning with
fever one minute, shaking with chills the next, she changed
to her sodden disguise, and lay down in the dismal glade.

Three days passed before she was able to move. Guided

by the booming of the Confederate guns, she pushed through the swamp and late in the afternoon reached a small white house. She tried the door, found it unlocked and entered a deserted hallway. But for a single occupant, the house was abandoned. On a straw tick in the living room lay a half-starved rebel soldier, near death from typhoid.

Emma Edmonds tended the sick man. She found tea, salt, and cornmeal, made a hoecake and fed him sparingly. The youth told her that he was Allan Hall. He asked her to deliver his gold watch to Major McKee of Elwell's staff. He died at midnight. Her vigil ended, she closed his eyes, shrouded him in his blanket, and fell asleep, heedless of the corpse by her side.

With morning another search disclosed mustard and pepper, a pair of old green spectacles, and a bottle of red ink. There was always the possibility of her running into some spy, as she had at Yorktown. This time she would be recognized. Her disguise, she decided, must be improved.

"Of the mustard, I made a strong plaster about the size of a dollar," she wrote. "I tied it on one side of my face. It blistered thoroughly. I cut off the blister and put on a large patch of black courtplaster. With the ink, I painted red lines about my eyes, and after giving my pale complexion a deep tinge with some ochre which I found in a closet, I put on my green glasses and my Irish hood, which came over my face about six inches and left for the nearest picket line. I felt perfectly safe for the watch was sufficient passport in daylight and a message to Major McKee would assure me courtesy at least."

As she neared the outpost she gave a final touch to her preparations. Rubbing black pepper in her eyes to turn them red and watery, she signalled the advance picket guard. A square of cotton window curtain served as a flag of truce. He was a jovial, apple-cheeked Englishman, ready to turn a receptive ear to another from the British Isles. He passed her without hesitation, warning her that the bridges across the Chickahominy had been completed, and that an attack was coming. He went on to tell her the number of hidden batteries they had prepared, and even indicated one concealed behind a brush heap by the roadside.

By the time she reached McKee's headquarters, she was five miles from the white farmhouse and the corpse of Allan Hall. The major was on a scouting expedition and due to return at nightfall. She found a simple ointment for her blistered face, for the sore was becoming infected, and spent the day peddling her wares throughout the camp.

One cannot help but wonder at the careless talk that went on behind the lines of both North and South. Today there would be the strictest watch on any stranger attempting to come into camp, and loose talk would bring a severe reprimand, if not punishment. But neither side was experienced in the ways of war. Espionage was in its swaddling clothes. Secret agents wandered across lines and military secrets became common property of the enemy. By nightfall, Emma Edmonds knew not only the location of each hidden battery, the number of men and their distribution, but the general strategy of the forthcoming battle as well.

Ushered before McKee, she told her story, presenting him with her credentials. The major wept. Captain Allan Hall she learned was his dearest friend. He offered her a federal ten-dollar bill. When she refused it, his grief turned to suspicion.

"Oh, General, forgive me," Emma wept, realizing how close she was to discovery, "but me conshins wud niver give me pace in this world nor in the next were I to take money for carryin' the dyin' message for that swate boy that's dead and gone, God rest his soul. Niver cud I do such a mane thing, if I am a poor woman."

She offered to lead a party to the body if they would furnish her a mount. Major McKee sent a detachment with her, but darkness fell before they had covered the five miles of rough road. The sergent in charge stationed pickets at all approaches and told a squad to get the body.

Emma Edmonds rode away, not to stop until she was safe behind the Union lines. This time she returned with a rebel horse as proof of her adventure.

Emma Edmonds undertook nine other spy trips. Her first experience at hard labor cured her of posing as a man, but she often appeared as an Irish biddy, though her makeup in this character was never twice the same. She altered each disguise so skillfully that not once during those eleven missions was she in real danger of discovery. Her final adventure was by far her most successful.

When the Union forces occupied Louisville, Emma Edmonds was promoted from a spy to a detective. She continued to carry on in disguise just as she had before, though now she worked within her own lines. The countryside was shot with Southern spies, radicals, and copperheads. It was her task to run them down. Except that help was near at hand, she was in danger every minute for the underground was vicious.

One of Louisville's leading merchants was especially outspoken. He hated the North and resented the Yankees who occupied the area. Because his employees feared trouble with northern authorities, they soon left his store. So when a personable "young man" approached him for a job, the merchant put him to work.

The new clerk was neatly dressed, quiet, and self-possessed. He said he was a foreigner who had gone south to observe the war at close range, and that he was in need of ready cash. He was an efficient young chap and proved himself to be a go-getter for business. He suggested peddling notions to the soldiers. He packed an assortment of pocket knives, suspenders, and the like, and returned each night for more. At the end of two weeks he had not only insured his job but had clues to three Southern spies in the very heart of the Union forces.

Confident that she must strike boldly, Emma Edmonds took another tack. She told her employer she believed the North was wrong. Defeat of the South meant disaster for the entire nation. She said she wanted to enlist under the Stars and Bars. The merchant listened and was convinced. He decided she should go through the lines with "a Union man who had taken the oath of allegiance (with crossed fingers)." He was really a rebel spy.

The attempt was set for the next night. She needed more time to perfect her plans. But is was tomorrow or not at all. She volunteered for a final peddling expedition, loaded herself with wares and contacted the Provost Marshal. He promised to visit the store for final instructions.

Next day Emma Edmonds was introduced to the man who would guide her to the Confederate ranks. A well-known resident of Louisville, above any suspicion, he mingled not only with the enlisted men but entertained officers as well.

Realizing that silence was safest, she assumed the embarrassment of a green country boy in the presence of his betters. The merchant gave a splendid sales talk and the deal was made. The Provost Marshal wandered in during the afternoon to make a small purchase and Emma slipped him a note.

Nine o'clock came—nine o'clock on a dark night, a night ideal for running lines. As the two headed southward, the clerk's embarrassment turned to open admiration for his guide. He, in turn, mellowing in the glow of such praise, talked at length about his activities in the secret service. He disclosed the identity of the other two suspects. One was a sutler, a man who followed the troops selling food and liquor; the other, a photographer who spent his time posing the Union generals. He was still in the midst of his recital when a detachment of Union cavalry swooped down and took them prisoners. Back at headquarters, rebel papers found on him left no doubt that he was a Southern spy.

The spy was shot at daybreak. The sutler was seized and given similar punishment. Warned in time, the photographer fled to safety.

Two years of trying service had taken their toll of Emma Edmonds. She had participated in both Battles of Bull Run. She was at Williamsburg, Fair Oaks, the Seven Days in front of Richmond, Antietam, and Fredericksburg. Besides playing nurse and spy, she served between times as an orderly, notably at the battle of Hanover Court House. She was at Vicksburg when it fell, once more in nurse's uniform.

There her strength failed. She fell ill with fever but struggled on until they carried her to the hospital.

"All my soldierly qualities seemed to have fled," she wrote. "I could do nothing but weep, hour after hour."

They gave her a certificate of disability. They commended her for her heroic service. They placed her Confederate carbine with other war trophies in Washington. And she retired to her New England home to record her experiences in *Nurse and Spy.*

And then they promptly forgot her. Except for her own book and notes in the war records at Washington, all too little recalls the accomplishments of the greatest woman spy of the Civil War—Emma Edmonds.

CHAPTER THREE

The Prisoner in the Legation

It was a typical autumn evening in London, rainy and foggy. The month was October, and the year 1896. A young Chinese stepped out of the train at Euston Station. Only a few hours earlier he had left the *Majestic*, when she docked in Liverpool. Throughout the long voyage from New York, this passenger had kept to himself. He seemed lost in his own thoughts.

In his early twenties, the young Chinese did not appear strange on the streets of London. Many people from the Orient came to the world's largest city to study, to learn English and to find work. He wore a well-cut suit, a neat little mustache and his hair was clipped close to his round head. His walk was firm, like that of a soldier.

For so young a man, the visitor had seen many adventures. He had circled the world, fleeing from his native country and the anger of his Emperor. Now he was in London with still more excitement ahead. He hailed a cab and asked the driver to take him to a hotel in the Strand district.

His room was pleasant and the people courteous and kind. In spite of the rain, he decided to look up a former teacher, Dr. James Cantlie, once head of the Medical College in Hong Kong.

The Cantlies greeted their visitor with warmth. They had a great deal to talk about, especially mutual friends who no longer wrote to England from China. The Oriental explained that many, like himself, were not in favor with the Emperor and had either been forced to leave China or were imprisoned.

"However," he said as he was leaving, "I intend to make a visit to the Chinese Legation in the near future . . . just to pay my respects."

Mr. Cantlie looked grave. "You'd better stay away from there," he warned. "They might kidnap you and ship you back to China."

During the following days, the youth fitted into the life of London as if he had been born there. His dress was English, his language was perfect and his good manners won him many new friends.

Dr. Henry Manson, another old friend, gave him the same warning as Dr. Cantlie. "Stay away from the Chinese Legation." The young man did not take the advice seriously. True, he might be wanted in China, but he was halfway around the world from his angry Emperor. Nothing could happen to him in friendly London.

A week after his arrival, he had moved from his hotel into a small, cozy apartment on Grey's Inn Road.

The next day was Sunday. He left his rooms and started out for Devonshire Street where he was to meet the Cantlies and go with them to church. When he reached Oxford Circus, he had the strange feeling he was being followed. The Chinese Legation was not far away.

Pausing to look around, he saw a Chinese in a mandarin robe standing only a few feet away. With a polite smile the older man addressed the student. "Are you a citizen of Japan or China, sir?"

"Of China," said the student.

"Of what part of China, may I ask?"

"Canton."

"That makes us compatriots. We speak the same dialect. I, too, am from Canton," said the unknown, speaking in Chinese.

The two strolled on together now, talking in their native language. They reached Cavendish Street. Suddenly another Chinese, also in mandarin clothing, made his appearance. Quietly, as though it were the most natural thing in the world, he joined the party, walking on the left side of the Chinese student.

The conversation went on, still in the politest Cantonese. The new member of the party invited his two countrymen to his room for tea.

"I'm very sorry to have to refuse your invitation," the student said. "I am on the way to meet some friends. We're going to church. Another time, perhaps."

Seemingly from nowhere a third Chinese appeared. The face of this man was unattractive. He looked capable of any brutality. The student's new acquaintances dropped their pretense of politeness. They seized their victim by his arms, steered him around a corner. There it was—the Chinese

Legation. A door opened. The student was hustled up the stairs and into the hallway.

He had not yet completely grasped the situation. It had all happened so quickly, in broad daylight and in the calm of a London Sunday. Could it be that the Chinese Secret Service had finally caught up with him, after he had put half the world between them and himself?

He was taken to a huge room full of costly furniture, locked in and left alone.

Two hours later he was led to another room. Two Chinese came and searched him. Most of his belongings were taken away, even the watch in his pocket. He was transferred to another room, this time on the third floor. The small windows were heavily barred. The view was of rooftops, chimney pots, fog and smoke.

The prisoner marvelled at the speed and smoothness with which the kidnapping had taken place. The door was unbolted. A tall, white-haired Englishman entered the "cell." Much later the student learned that he was Sir Halliday Macartney, a lawyer who worked for the Chinese Government as counsellor and adviser.

"My dear young man," he began, "you are now on Chinese territory. To all intents and purposes you are in China, under Chinese law. May I have your name?"

The exile gave him it.

The Britisher smiled faintly. "We know better. Your name is Sun Wen." It was the name the student had used signing petitions for reform, political pamphlets and manifestos. "No sense beating about the bush, my dear young man," the Britisher continued. "We have been fully informed about your movements. We had a message from the United States telling us that you were arriving on the *Majestic*. The Chinese Minister has requested your arrest."

"May I ask why?"

"You know only too well. You have displeased your Emperor and your Government."

The prisoner remained silent. He had acted on his deep beliefs. He also knew his Government thought he had done a crime.

The Britisher continued his accusations. For a man so thoroughly western in appearance, he was certainly a loyal slave of his Chinese employer.

"Sun Wen, you drew up a petition calling for a widespread reform program. You requested that it be presented to the Emperor."

"I did."

"We in London have been ordered to detain you until we find out the Emperor's personal wishes."

The prisoner could only too vividly imagine what form the Emperor's pleasure would take. He saw a headsman and a gleaming sword blade.

"May I inform my English friends of my presence at the Legation?"

"No, you cannot. You may, however, write a letter to your landlord instructing him to release your belongings, which will then be brought to you."

The prisoner wrote a note to his landlord. That was all

Sir Halliday cared to say to him. He strolled out of the room and left the young man to his thoughts.

In the notes he made during his imprisonment, he recorded this comment:

"It was very evident that my questioner was playing a sly game to get hold of my belongings, especially my papers, in the hope of finding correspondence, to learn who my Chinese helpers were."

An hour later he was startled by a fearful noise. Carpenters were installing a second lock on his door. In addition two guards were being ordered to stand in front of his door at all times. Hearing the guards conversing in Cantonese, the prisoner tried to speak to them through the door. They did not reply but entered the room and searched him again. This time they took away his keys and pocket knife.

In the late afternoon the guards asked him what he wanted to eat. He asked only for a glass of milk. At seven, two English servants came to clean his room and bring coal and wood for the fireplace. Evidently they had strict orders. They acted as if the room were empty.

He passed a restless night. Though the room was provided with a comfortable bed, he did not bother to undress. He could hear the guards talking, and from outside the windows the night noises of the city, the sound of trotting cab horses, the clatter of hoofs and rolling of wheels on cobblestones. Unwelcome thoughts crowded his mind. He was not afraid to die, but not this way — in a trap. Why did Macartney, an Englishman of high position, care to serve a cruel Emperor?

The next morning found the prisoner looking pale and tired. His mind, however, was sharper than it had been the previous day. He was determined to find a way to escape. He would try bribery. Above all, he must play for time. His friends had cautioned him not to go near the Legation. When they realized that he was missing, they would know where to look.

His first visitor that day was Kidnapper No. 1, the man who had first spoken to him on the street. He gave his name as Tang and said he was one of the many secretaries of the Imperial Chinese Legation. Tang said, "I now come to talk to you as a friend. You had better confess that you are Sun Wen. There is no sense denying it. All arrangements have been made for your return to China. You are well known at home. The Emperor and the Tsung-Li-Yamen know your activities. Just think what a wonderful chance you'll have to distinguish yourself, what a beautiful ending for a career, what an example you will be able to give by dying courageously. You will become a real hero."

"Why do you think I am going to die?" asked the prisoner. "After all, I am not in China, but in England, a free country. What can you do to me here? Of course you can kill me here in the Legation. That is certainly something you can easily do. But without a trial, such an act would be considered murder. These things have a way of leaking out. You wouldn't want any trouble with the British authorities. Then again, you might try to have me sent home for trial. Such a procedure takes a long time. Besides, the British Government would learn of my illegal imprisonment. I don't think the English would turn me over to you anyway— this country has a tradition for providing political asylum and protection."

A sneer appeared on the face of the Legation secretary.

"Naturally we won't ask for extradition—that would be a very stupid thing to do. A freighter is waiting for you in Southampton. We will have no trouble at all in doping you and transferring you from the Legation building to the ship. After that you will be put in chains. Before the ship reaches Hong Kong it will be met by a gunboat which will take you to Canton. That is where your execution will take place."

"Without a trial, I suppose," the prisoner said dryly.

"The proper formalities will be observed. We are not barbarians, you know. First the trial and then the beheading," the middle-aged official answered politely.

"Don't you think you are running a risk? What if the British police should get to know of this thing? I might get word out or try to escape. Then you'd all be in hot water."

Tang assured his prisoner that this chance was extremely remote. He was well guarded, and there would be no slip-up.

"Have you forgotten about the officers and crew of the ship which is supposed to take me back?" asked the prisoner. "They will know something is going on. The docks are filled with people. They're bound to notice something and make a stir."

Tang seemed unmoved. "Everything had been thought of," he said. The owners of the ship were close friends of Sir Halliday Macartney. They were interested in trade with China. He had their word for it that nothing would happen.

The more the prisoner talked with Tang, the more he learned of the plot. This could certainly be useful. Tang seemed pleased to discuss the arrangements. He was sure the situation was under control. For example, Tang told him that he would "travel" on one of the Glen Line steamers during the coming week. The Minister had not been willing to charter a ship exclusively for the purpose of carrying him to justice.

The prisoner pointed out that the plan looked rather difficult and complicated. One misstep and the whole thing would fall through. Hadn't they better change their minds and set him free?

Tang did not seem to appreciate this kind of humor. Not a muscle of his face moved as he replied: "You understand the problem very well. You are a clever man. Too bad you are not loyal to us. As it happens, you are right. We are not very pleased with this plan. If we had our way, we would dispose of you here in the Legation. That is a far more practical way of doing it. But our orders are to have you sent to China. The Emperor wishes it."

The prisoner's diary records more of this fateful conversation:

"For my information and consolation, Tang then cited the case of a Korean patriot who, escaping from Korea to Japan, was convinced by a countryman he should go to Shanghai. He was put to death in the British concession. His dead body was sent back to the Chinese to Korea for 'punishment.' On arrival there, it was beheaded. The murderer was rewarded and given an important political post. Tang evidently hoped he would also be promoted by his Government for arresting me and securing my death. I asked him why he was so cruel. He replied: 'This is by order of the Emperor who wants you captured at any price, preferably alive.' "

The prisoner remained calm. He continued to discuss various possibilities. "If the British Government should get to know of this plot, it might declare all members of this Legation unwelcome in London. In that case you would have to return to China. My people in the province of Kwang-Tung would be on the lookout for a chance to revenge me. I hate to think what they would do to you and your entire family in payment for your act of treachery."

This threat found its mark. Family feuds and bloody acts of revenge were very real in Tang's mind. He became apologetic and anxious to prove to the prisoner that he was only obeying orders. He was but a minor official—he had to do as his superiors commanded, even if he did not like his assignments. He asked for understanding and forgiveness. In fact, he offered the young man a helpful suggestion.

"As I see it, you still have a small chance for life. You must deny that you had anything to do with the Canton plot and the reform plans. Accuse your accusers. Say that the whole thing is a trap sprung by the mandarins. Declare that you came voluntarily to the Legation to clear yourself and to ask for a review of your case."

Since no other course was open, the prisoner agreed to write such a letter. Perhaps it would soften the hearts of his kidnappers. Tang took the letter with a peculiar smile. It was the last time the prisoner saw him.

As the days went by, the young man realized he had fallen into a trap. He'd been foolish to write such a letter. It acknowledged he had come to the Legation of his own accord. This would clear the Legation with the British authorities.

As time ran out, he was ready to try anything to reach the outside world. On two occasions he tried to smuggle notes to his friends, but none of the servants could be bribed. He wrote short notes on tiny bits of paper and threw them out the window in the hope that some passerby would find them. The first ones were caught in the wind, tossed up and whirled about for a moment. He watched them fall into a drain pipe on the roof below.

He wrote other notes and weighted them with copper coins to make sure they would fall to the street. One fell into the garden of the adjoining house. Another note fell on the roof on the other side. The third and last fell on the street. It was spotted by the Legation guards.

That was the end of the prisoner's attempt to draw attention to his plight. Some servants entered his room and fastened wooden boards over his windows. The room was now in total darkness.

"I was worse off than ever," wrote the young man. "My only means of communication with the outside world was gone."

The prisoner had been raised as a Christian, and he found consolation in prayer. He spent many hours praying. At least it seemed hours, for he had no way of estimating time. He didn't know whether one day went by or many. It was perpetual night in his room and blackest night in his soul. His only light came from the fire.

He had one last chance. He could appeal to the English servant who appeared to clean his room, bring him wood and tend the fire. He performed his duties like a machine, never speaking nor seeming to see him. His name was Edward Cole.

One morning the prisoner spoke to the man.

"Sir, will you not do something for me?" he asked.

To call a servant "sir" was unusual. Edward looked at the prisoner as though seeing him for the first time. "Who are you?" he asked in a low, frightened voice. "And what do you want of me?"

"I am a political refugee from China. I came to England to seek the protection of the British Government. I am a Christian just like yourself. You must have read in the newspapers that the Sultan of Turkey is massacring the Armenian Christians. Well, the Emperor of China wants to kill me because I am a Christian. I belong to a political party that wants good government and democratic freedom for all in China, the way it is in England. I have done no harm to anyone—I was brought here by trickery and am being held against my will."

It was rash of him to say as much as he did, but he felt it was the only way to win the man's sympathy.

Cole did not answer immediately. He busied himself sweeping the floor and hearth. At last he said in a whisper, "I don't know whether the British Government would want to help you. After all, you are a foreigner."

The prisoner replied, "The British Government would surely help me. That is why I am being kept here by force. Otherwise the Chinese Government would have to ask for my official extradition."

The servant went on with his work. There was no way of telling whether he felt sympathetic, or whether the prisoner's plea fell on deaf ears. "My life is in your hands, sir," the prisoner pleaded. "If the proper authorities are informed, I shall be saved. Otherwise, it means death for me. Is it not better to save a life than to see it destroyed? Doesn't your duty as a Christian come before your duty to your employers?"

Cole had never been appealed to in such terms before. He had always been a good, conscientious servant. He was not concerned in the business of his superiors.

He finished his work and withdrew without a word.

It was another sleepless night for the prisoner. Had he won Cole over — or would Cole go to his employers and reveal their conversation?

In the morning Cole brought the prisoner his breakfast. He deposited it on the table and left. Returning in the evening with a scuttle of coal, the servant again had nothing to say. Instead, he pointed towards the scuttle he had brought in and left the room.

Tucked in among the coals was a scrap of white paper. The prisoner snatched it up and read:

"I am willing to take a letter to one of your friends, but not to the police. You must not write at the table. The guards can see through the keyhole. If you write on your bed, you cannot be seen from the hall."

The prisoner lay down on his bed and faced the wall. With a tiny stub of a pencil he wrote a message on a visiting card:

To Dr. James Cantlie
46 Devonshire Street

Please take care of the messenger for me. He is very poor and will lose his work by doing this for me. I was kidnapped into the Chinese Legation on Sunday and shall be smuggled out from England to China for death. Pray rescue me. A ship is already chartered by C. L. to take me to China.

But the note was not delivered as its writer had written it. Cole waited until October 17, a Saturday and his day off. Being careful, he did not deliver the prisoner's note, but sent one of his own by messenger. It read:

There is a friend of yours imprisoned in the Chinese Legation since last Sunday. They intend to send him out to China where it is certain they will execute him. It is very sad for the poor man. Unless something is done at once he will be taken away and no one will know it. I dare not sign my name but this is the truth, so believe what I say. Whatever you do must be done at once or it will be too late. His name is, I believe, Lin Yen Sen.

The Cantlies were enjoying a typical Saturday night at home, reading by the fireplace when this letter arrived. They had missed their Chinese friend, but they knew that Orientals often acted oddly by English standards. They were sure he would turn up with a perfectly good explanation for his behavior.

When the note arrived, Cantlie knew that he had to act quickly. Being a professor of medicine, he knew little about investigations, spies, kidnapping or politics. But he knew that Sir Halliday Macartney was the legal counsel for the Chinese Government. He decided to see him first. It never occurred to him to go directly to the police. He also knew

Sir Halliday lived nearby, in an impressive four-story building of grey stone. But the house was closed, the shades pulled down and the high iron gate locked. Perhaps its owner had gone to the country for the week end.

A constable on duty in nearby Marylebone Road informed the doctor the house had been closed for at least six months. At this point Dr. Cantlie decided to go to the nearest police station. There an inspector listened to his story and advised Cantlie to go to Scotland Yard.

The officers at police headquarters were polite. But the story was so fantastic, so implausible and un-English, that they began to imagine that the doctor must be a crank. They listened and took down the facts. They would, they assured Dr. Cantlie, report the matter to their superiors. That was as far as Dr. Cantlie got. Around midnight, he left and walked home.

There was not much Cantlie could do at that hour of the night. At eight o'clock the next morning he was out of his house, consulting a friend. The two men deliberated a long time. They decided that if Scotland Yard failed to act it might be wise to get someone to make a private visit to the Legation.

Once more Cantlie stopped at Macartney's house. He hoped to find at least the caretaker who would tell him how to get in touch with Sir Halliday. The place was completely deserted.

Finally Cantlie went home, exhausted from his long trip across London. He found Cole waiting for him in the living room, and heard the "wild story" from the man's own lips.

Cantlie told of his visits to the Macartney residence. Cole raised his eyebrows. Sir Halliday was living in town and was in the Legation every day. In his opinion Macartney had a large part in the incident.

Cantlie immediately saw that this complicated the matter. A man of Macartney's standing had great power and influence. At this point Cole volunteered further information. Macartney, he explained, had passed word around the Legation that the prisoner was a dangerous man, who was being kept under lock and key for his own good. He was due to be shipped home on Tuesday. A captain and some sailors had come to the Legation to discuss the matter.

That gave them only forty-eight hours in which to act. He set off immediately to see his medical colleague, Dr. Manson. Together they went to Scotland Yard to make another appeal for help.

The officer on duty listened to their story. He consulted the records. "You were here on Saturday night," he said. "No new facts have turned up since to confirm your story."

In desperation the two doctors decided to go directly to the Foreign Office. It was not far, but getting in was another story. They were politely informed that the clerk in charge could not see them before five in the afternoon.

They decided to wait. After several long hours, they were ushered into the office of the chief-in-charge. He heard them out and with a shrug of his shoulders regretfully informed the gentlemen that since the day was Sunday, no action could be taken. He would report the matter to his superiors early next morning.

The doctors were panicked! What if the Chinese should change their plans and ship the prisoner out a day earlier? They expressed anger: the entire British law enforcement system seemed to be in a state of paralysis because it was Sunday.

The Foreign Office official tried to explain this was a delicate matter involving foreign relations, diplomatic privileges, immunities and international law. He personally did not have the power to deal with such a problem. The doctors would have to wait.

The doctors, however, were not easily discouraged. They stood together outside the Foreign Office debating the next move.

Cantlie suggested he was too well known to go to the Chinese Legation, but there was no reason why Dr. Manson should not be admitted. If he were not back within an hour, Cantlie would inform Scotland Yard.

It was 6:30 p.m. when Dr. Manson rang the bell at No. 49 Portland Place. An English footman opened the door. Dr. Manson was led into an anteroom which was furnished with silver and gold brocades, bronze Buddhas and a huge portrait of the Emperor.

Dr. Manson asked to see one of the attachés on an urgent matter. He had not long to wait before Tang entered the room. Bowing and smiling, the Chinese greeted the Englishman who stated the reason for his visit.

"A friend of mine, one of my former medical students in China, is being held prisoner in this Legation. I demand to see him."

Tang's face became cold, stony and cruel.

"We have no prisoners in this Legation. What is the name of this young man you seek?"

"Sun Wen."

"No man of that name is under this roof."

"I know he is being held here. So does Scotland Yard and the Foreign Office."

Tang was unmoved. He assured his excited visitor it was all a great mistake. Perhaps someone was playing a joke on him. So convincing was the official's manner that Manson believed him. When he rejoined Dr. Cantlie thirty minutes later, Manson said the story really was a bit unbelievable. The people at the Legation knew nothing of the matter.

Dr. Cantlie, however, was more disturbed than ever. He could not agree with his friend's interpretation. In fact, he was convinced that the danger for his Chinese friend had increased as a result of the visit to the Legation. Something must be done quickly or the prisoner would be put on the boat, perhaps earlier than planned. Then and there Cantlie decided to put a private detective on the job—to keep watch on the Legation in case an attempt was made to remove the prisoner. But then he remembered it was Sunday, a Victorian Sunday. Nobody was available.

Cantlie went back to Scotland Yard and begged them to set some detective to watch the Legation. He was told the place was out of their zone; he was advised to go to the appropriate West End Police Station.

There the doctor experienced his usual trouble in making

the officers see that this was a real emergency. In the absence of concrete evidence, the police had no authority to place guards around the Chinese Legation. As a last resort, Cantlie offered money to any constable off duty who would undertake the watch as a private job. The officers at the station were on duty all night but they recommended a man who lived in Islington, a retired member of the force.

On his way to Islington Cantlie had to pass Fleet Street. Here he had an inspiration. He walked into the office of *The Times* and asked to see a member of the editorial staff.

Nobody showed any eagerness to help him. The clerk in the front office insisted that the gentleman state the reason for an interview. Fuming with impatience, Cantlie took the slip of paper from the clerk and wrote these words:

> Brutal kidnapping at the Chinese Legation; immediate danger of death.

The receptionist was dumbfounded. It was not every day that visitors came with such messages. But the person who could help was not available until ten in the evening. "Come back then," the clerk said.

"I will," Cantlie said grimly.

At Islington the doctor found the retired member of the constabulary had something else he had to do that night. He promised, however, to find a substitute.

By this time Dr. Cantlie was dead tired, but he returned to *The Times* office where a veteran journalist listened to his story. He admitted it was an astonishing story. Still, it was of such importance and delicacy that the reporter was unable to do anything until it was referred to the editorial board.

Dr. Cantlie left in utter disgust. He had knocked at every possible door and been turned away.

It was eleven-thirty when he arrived home. Tired as he was, he was in no mood for sleep. His wife tried to calm him. "Perhaps something will suggest itself in the morning," Mrs. Cantlie said.

But this only made the doctor more restless. He couldn't go to sleep while that young man might be being murdered. In the course of his work as a doctor, he had learned the value of persistence. One had to go on trying.

Dr. Cantlie decided to skip sleep. He put on some warmer clothes and set out for the Chinese Legation. He would watch it himself. He stayed there until the following morning and then paid a visit to Salter's Detective Agency as soon as it opened. There he engaged a number of agents to watch the Chinese Legation day and night.

His next call was to the Foreign Office. He told his story once more, this time in the form of a sworn statement. The reaction was not too encouraging. Officials pointed out that the only evidence was the prisoner's own note claiming he had been kidnapped. The rest was hearsay and could be very regrettable, if it turned out to be a false rumor.

The Foreign office, however, asked Scotland Yard to investigate whether the Chinese Legation had chartered a ship.

The answer came promptly. Such a charter had been drawn up with the Glen Line for a ship to leave on Tuesday. The vessel was to carry a mixed cargo to China. There was also to be one passenger. His name was not given; he was merely identified as a Chinese national.

In the meantime the young man held behind the windows of the Chinese Legation was dying all the deaths which uncertainty can produce. He had no idea whether Cole could be trusted to have passed his message to Dr. Cantlie.

The first real gleam of hope came when Cole brought in the usual evening scuttle of coal. In it was a note: "Be hopeful. We are working for you."

Still, this was no assurance the rescuers would make it in time. Cole sent another note to Dr. Cantlie:

I shall have a good opportunity to let your friend out on the roof of the next house in Portland Place tonight. Have someone there waiting to receive him. If I am able to do it, find means to let me know.

Cantlie hurried to Scotland Yard with a plea to have them put some police officers on the roof of the neighboring house. But the police decided against it. The proper legal steps had been taken, and soon the order would come through for the Legation to open its doors for inspection.

On October 22, England's great contribution to the rights of man, the writ of habeas corpus, was requested for an unknown prisoner. (This is an order issued by a judge to produce a prisoner for trial and to state the reasons for keeping him.) But unfortunately the judge before whom the application was made refused to grant it.

Nevertheless it brought England's newspapers into the fight. A reporter from the *Globe* called on Cantlie for a story and the doctor gave him the facts. He also spoke of his unsuccessful visits to *The Times*.

That was the turning point. Other newspapers became interested in the prisoner in the Legation. Soon reporters were swarming outside the house in Portland Place. They demanded to see the prisoner. Secretary Tang came out of his private office to talk to the reporters. Polite, smiling, he assured the gentlemen the story was a gigantic hoax put across by some joker with a wild imagination.

The reporters warned Tang that if the prisoner were not released within a day, citizens might storm the Legation.

Tang went on smiling. It was apparent that he failed to measure the temper of the people of London, or the influence of the national press.

Finally newspapermen tracked down Sir Halliday Macartney to Midland House. The *Daily Mail* pulled off the scoop and printed the first interview with the legal representative of the Chinese Legation.

INTERVIEWS WITH SIR HALLIDAY MACARTNEY

Sir Halliday Macartney, Counsellor of the Chinese Legation, visited the Foreign Office at 3:30 yesterday afternoon. In conversation with a press representative Sir Halliday said, "I am unable to give you any information beyond what has already appeared in print." On being informed that the Foreign Office had just issued an announcement to the effect that Lord Salisbury had requested the Chinese

Minister to release the prisoner, Sir Halliday admitted that this was so. In answer to a further question as to what would be the result of the request, replied, "The man will be released.

"Sun Wen is not the name of the man whom we have upstairs. We know his real identity and his movements since he set foot in England. He came of his own free will to the Legation. He was not kidnapped into the premises. It is quite a usual thing for a lone Chinese in London to call here to chat with a countryman. There appears to be some ground for suspecting that this visitor came with some idea of spying on us."

By October 23 Lord Salisbury, Britain's Foreign Minister, issued a note of protest to the Chinese Minister demanding the immediate release of the prisoner.

Later, the Legation guards came to "Sun Wen," told him to put on his shoes, coat and hat and to follow them downstairs. Was this the last act of his kidnapping? Were the Chinese ready to ship him out? Or was he going to be transferred to a cellar, where he would be shot?

"Where are we going?" he asked his Chinese guards. There was no answer.

The prisoner was led downstairs into a small reception room. Three men were waiting for him. One was a friend—Dr. Cantlie. Accompanying the doctor was an inspector of Scotland Yard, and a clerk from the Foreign Office.

The doors were open. The four men walked out of the Legation, where a huge crowd was massed to greet the prisoner. The young man who had landed on England's shore so quietly three weeks before, was now bombarded with hundreds of questions. "How did you manage to reach the doctor?" But this was one question the ex-prisoner would not answer. He had an obligation to the loyal servant who had saved his life.

After a visit to Scotland Yard and a happy dinner at the Cantlie home, the free man wrote a letter of gratitude to every London newspaper. The text of the letter made history:

Will you kindly express through your columns my deep appreciation of the action of the British Government in effecting my release from the Chinese Legation? I also thank the press for their timely help and sympathy. If anything were needed to convince me of the generous public spirit which pervades Great Britain and the love of justice which distinguishes its people, the recent acts of the last few days have done so.

Knowing and feeling more keenly than ever what a constitutional Government and enlightened people mean, I am prompted to pursue still more actively the cause of advancement, education and civilization in my own well-beloved but oppressed country.

Yours faithfully,
Sun Yat Sen.*

The man who wrote this letter later became the first President of the Republic of China and the pioneer of Chinese democracy.

---

* (Sun Yat Sen became China's great leader dedicated to overthrowing the Manchu regime and establishing a republic. He was the son of a poor Chinese farmer and became associated with a secret revolutionary society. The failure of a plot led to the execution of several of the conspirators, but Sun Yat Sen escaped. A reward for his capture was offered, but in 1912 he became provisional President of the new republic. He died in 1925.)

CHAPTER FOUR

The Man with the Red Beard

The main characteristic that comes to mind when one thinks of a secret agent is secrecy; and we all associate heroism with a manly modesty. The tale told in this chapter, however, is of an agent who was about as conspicuous as possible—both in appearance and personality; and, though he has performed, as far as can be ascertained, a great many deeds of daring and heroism, he is also rather prone to recount them, possibly with embellishments.

Here is an exploit of Captain Dod Orsborne—Le Capitaine Solitaire—sometime of His Majesty's Navy, always in trouble, and the possessor of one of the most magnificent beards of modern times, a bright red one.

On June 10, 1935, a slim, well-groomed blond woman boarded the Munich express at the Anhalter Bahnhof in Berlin and went to a first-class compartment. In Munich she changed to the Rome express.

A cosmopolitan type, there was nothing to stamp her as English, Scandinavian or German. She kept aloof from the other passengers. As the train came near the Italian border, a group of uniformed officials squeezed into her compartment. The lady showed her British passport which gave her name as Miss Helen Holborn.

Another passenger on the same train attracted attention. According to his passport, his name was Fernando Queseda and he was born in Barcelona. He was a Spaniard, with gleaming black hair, olive complexion, graceful body, large nose and long, thin hands. He said his only cash was ten marks in change.

When asked to open his bags, the customs men found an elegant wardrobe, many silk shirts, a variety of perfumes, and a traveling kit trimmed with silver. The customs official searched no further. The man's air of assurance put them off. In any case, he was traveling first-class.

In Rome the travelers scattered in all directions.

The following evening the Englishwoman arrived at Parker's Hotel in Naples, a quiet aristocratic place much used by English visitors to the city. The management took the lady's passport, as Italian police regulations prescribed. She went immediately to her room. The following evening, dressed in a simple blue suit and carrying a bouquet of white carnations, she left the hotel. When she got into the taxi, she asked the porter to interpret for her. The porter told the driver to take her into town.

On the edge of the city boundary she left the taxi and walked to a restaurant in the little, old port of Naples. This restaurant, Ci Teresa, was filled with a colorful crowd. The lady lingered at the entrance. One of the waiters saw the bouquet of white carnations, and rushed to her.

"Unfortunately, there is no table where you can sit alone, but if you do not mind . . ." He led her to a table set off in one corner.

At the dimly lit table a gentleman was sitting alone. He rose at once. He would be honored, he said. The lady sat down. The headwaiter reappeared, leading another guest to the table. This was none other than Fernando Queseda, who had traveled on the same train as Miss Holborn from Munich, Germany to Rome. The three had not met before, but each knew about the others. They talked in low tones.

Miss Holborn's real name was Angelica Dubrow. A German, she was an agent of the Gestapo's newly established Spanish section, the very existence of which was a closely guarded secret even within the Gestapo itself. Of Baltic descent, Helen had entered the profession of espionage at a comparatively early age and had served the government in an international counterfeiting case. At that time she was known by another name. She had not come from England, nor had she passed the Dutch-German border as her passport indicated. These fake entries had been made to enable her to carry a large sum of foreign currency.

Fernando Queseda was more practiced in the espionage profession. However, he had one disadvantage which caused him trouble. His picture had once appeared in a newspaper in connection with a well-known scandal. A Spanish businessman had tried to bribe a Spanish president for permission to start a gambling casino on Malorca. Queseda had also been involved in smuggling American cigarettes into Spain.

The third and newest spy was Gaston d'Ette, an Italian. He entered his profession only after Mussolini had come to power.

Each of these persons had been carefully selected by the three secret services. They each had special qualifications. General Francisco Franco, one-time chief of the Spanish general staff in Madrid, and now assured of the personal loyalty of the Spanish troops in Morocco, was already making the first moves in the game that was to raise him to mastery of all Spain.

Spain and Franco were the subjects of the conversation at the table in the Restaurant Ci Teresa in Naples.

General Franco and those who stood behind him had put over a remarkable coup. They had persuaded both the German and the Italian governments to something that was very much in their own interests.

Since there now existed a Fascist Germany and a Fascist Italy, Franco said the power of Fascism in Europe would be immensely strengthened if a Fascist regime could be set up in Spain.

To this end, the Spanish conspirators proposed that Berlin and Rome secretly send an air fleet to Spanish Morocco. With its help Franco would be able to seize power in Spain in one quick blow. With eighty planes—a powerful force in those days—the regiments of the Spanish foreign legion, who loved Franco, their former chief, together with native African Moors, could speedily attack any spot in Spain.

Berlin and Rome approved the proposal. Payment for the planes was guaranteed by a number of Spanish industrialists. The eighty planes were to be shipped from Germany to Italy. Italian factories would supply the engines.

But how could these planes be sent to Morocco? It was out of the question to fly them there. Even to fly them one at a time would attract too much attention. The power of Britain counted for something, and since the British were unfriendly to Franco there might be trouble if they got wind of the move. It was therefore decided to crate the eighty planes and ship them secretly to Spanish Morocco.

The crates would then be shipped by ordinary freighters to Naples. There they would be transferred to small Italian vessels and sent on to their destination. They would be labeled "toys" from Nuremberg and "small assorted ironware" from Sollingen, and addressed to a firm in Naples. This firm would charter the vessels for trans-shipment.

The other two agents at the table listened with growing excitement. The Spaniard grimly told them that all these arrangements would have to be changed. The plan to send the crates to Spanish Morocco aboard small freighters was out of the question.

"What do you mean? We can't change our plans now," Gaston d'Ette protested.

The Spaniard explained. "A mysterious ship," he said, "has been raising the devil in the vicinity of the ports where the crates are to be landed. In fact, the ship has been causing trouble at every important point along the Moroccan coast. The captain is called Le Capitaine Solitaire because he is always alone. He is usually met in waters that are just barely navigable. No one knows his employer but the chances are that he works for the British Secret Service."

Queseda explained further how the mysterious captain had turned up in June. Since his appearance nothing that happened in Morocco could be kept secret. Small radios were working in the area, sending messages to the British Secret

Service. If those planes were shipped to Spanish Morocco, he added with a sad attempt at humor, it might turn out to be a season of many shipwrecks.

"Well, how do you think we can arrange it?" Fraulein Dubrow demanded.

Senor Queseda proposed that the Italian Government take the bull by the horns, rush the crates to the nearest airplane factory and have the planes assembled. German and Italian pilots could then fly them to Spanish Morocco.

The Italian, Gaston d'Ette, blew up. "My country cannot do anything of the sort," he retorted.

Fraulein Drubrow had an inspiration.

"Our problem is to ship a mountain of crates to a certain place without attracting attention, and then to assemble the planes," she said. "There are places under the Italian flag that are not in Europe. What about the Libyan desert, for example? A temporary factory could be set up there, near a port, and the planes assembled. They could be flown by night along southern routes to Spanish Morocco. Nobody would be the wiser."

The three agents passed this suggestion on to their superiors. All three governments thought well of it. The Italians pointed out that near the small port of Zuara, fifty miles west of Tripoli, there already existed an army repair shop for the servicing of military planes. This would serve admirably as an assembly plant. The situation was ideal—out of the town, in the middle of the desert, and therefore easy to guard.

The agents therefore arranged to transfer the crates to the small freighters in Naples. But the destination was changed from Spanish Morocco to Zuara. All seemed plain sailing.

The Spaniard and the Italian were ready to celebrate in advance. Fraulein Dubrow was more cautious. "Since we know who our enemy is," she said, "we have to keep an eye on him. How much do we know about this mysterious Capitaine Solitaire?"

"He is a British seaman," Queseda answered. "About thirty years old. Sometimes he wears a beard, sometimes he's beardless. When he is unshaved he can't be mistaken; his whiskers are red. But we know more about his ship than about him. It's about seventy-five feet in length, diesel-motored, funnel back of a low bridge, no masts—a typical smuggler's boat."

The information was not very satisfactory. Apparently the man could be identified only if he were with his boat, or if he were unshaven.

For the present the three agents had nothing to do in Naples but await the arrival of the "toys" and "ironware." They were quite unaware of something that had happened meantime at the port of Emden in Germany. While the planes were being loaded onto a freighter, a truck drove up to the pier. Beside the driver sat a man who was later described as wearing a light-colored raincoat, a hard hat and a pair of gold-rimmed glasses.

The man was equipped with all the proper papers. He insisted on adding another crate to those on the ship. The first mate argued angrily, but the stranger was calm. He seemed to know that no matter how much the first mate stormed, he would finally obey his company's written orders and take on the extra crate.

The crate was conspicuously marked with diagonal red lines and labeled in German and Italian, "Handle with care."

With the others, it was safely stowed away in the hold.

In the desert, at a place so lonely it seemed the end of the world, the Italian Army air base had been hastily prepared for assembling the expected air fleet. Barracks had been set up for the pilots, and security squads drafted. To make the place even more secure, barbed wire had been set around the entire area and a formation of Italian police, together with troops, had been ordered to reinforce the usual guards.

The tiny, insignificant town of Zuara itself had never seen a cargo as large as that brought in during the early part of July, 1935. The natives gaped and made wild guesses as to what could possibly be inside those crates. They were given no time to find out. As soon as the crates had been put ashore, they were loaded into big new trucks and vanished into the desert.

All three agents were at the port when the precious cargo arrived. They accompanied the crates to the air base itself and lived in the barracks while the "ironware" and "toys" were magically turned into airplanes. Their main thought was how soon they might get away from this dreary slice of desert.

Apart from their boredom, they had every reason to feel satisfied with themselves. Their work had earned them a handsome bonus. So far as they knew, no one suspected an airfleet lay inside those crates. The chance of any interference with the cargo seemed remote. Those planes were certain to arrive safely at their destination.

On August 16, 1935, towards evening, the chief of police called on the agents. He brought along a bottle of wine and they drank together.

"Anything going on at the port?" asked one of the agents.

"Not a thing," the chief replied. "Just a British fishing boat with a damaged motor that came in for repairs."

He was amazed at the effect of his remark.

"What's the length of that boat?" demanded his companions, obviously alarmed.

The chief, familiar with ships, was precise. "I'd put it at seventy-five feet," he said.

For a moment none dared ask what the captain looked like. At last the German agent, Fraulein Dubrow, put the question.

"A good-looking fellow," the chief replied. "Has a kind of reddish beard."

The three began yelling at him. He yelled back, assuring them that nothing had happened. The man was in the port and really did have a damaged ship. "I saw the damage myself. But if you want, we can go right over and arrest him."

They dashed to the chief's car and roared away to the port. There lay the boat. None had the slightest doubt it belonged to Capitaine Solitaire. They began discussing this next move. But at that moment something occurred that made all discussion pointless. Something happened that was talked of for years afterwards along the North Africa coast.

The silence was broken by a thunderous explosion, rapidly followed by several more. At the same time, back in the direction of the plane factory, yellow, white and red flames shot skyward. A pillar of fire lit up the evening desert and sent the natives of Zuara shrieking in terror.

The Italian and the Spaniard flung themselves into the car, dragging the unwilling Fraulein Dubrow with them. Madly they drove out over the desert toward the ominous glow.

When they arrived they found the factory in ruins. It was a sea of darting flames. Soldiers ran helplessly, aimlessly, achieving nothing.

The three angry agents almost gave the police chief a thrashing. He seemed strangely unmoved by the disaster. He escaped further punishment by a promise to arrest Capitaine Solitaire. Reaching the pier, he did not arrest the captain, but seized the boat and put two policemen aboard, ordering them to shoot at the slightest move to put the vessel to sea.

Then he rushed back to the fire and asked for further orders.

Two weeks later two upset Italian policemen called on the Italian Consul in the French port of Oran. They told a strange story. They said they had been told to guard a British fishing boat in the port of Zuara. While they were on board, the boat had suddenly put to sea, though they could not figure out how it was started. Seasick with the heaving of the boat, they were helpless as children. Their guns had been taken away and they expected to be dumped overboard. Instead, they had been put ashore at a lonely spot near Oran.

And that was how Capitaine Solitaire kept Franco from taking over Spain as early as 1935.

The Italian Government exiled its agent, Gaston d'Ette, to the Lipari islands. It was said that after six months he committed suicide.

What happened to the Spaniard, Fernando Queseda, is unknown. The German agent, Angelica Dubrow, was seen in Rio de Janeiro in 1938. She never returned to Germany.

CHAPTER FIVE

The Legend of Mata Hari

Margarida Gertrud Zelle, known as Mata Hari, the world's most famous woman spy, was born in Holland, August 7, 1876. As a girl of fourteen, she entered a Catholic convent. On a vacation at the Hague, when Margarida was sweet seventeen, she met Campbell MacLeod, a dashing captain in Holland's colonial forces.

Captain MacLeod was a good-for-nothing soldier of fortune who drank heavily, gambled and chased women as sport. But young Margarida, inexperienced in life and love outside the convent, was dazzled by his uniform and the exciting stories he told of his army adventures. Besides, the captain was forty, greying, and treated her like a kind father.

They were married. By 1895, the two were in Java, Indonesia, where three children were born to them. The captain soon tired of his young wife. He drank more than ever, was cruel and beat Margarida regularly. At times she feared for her life.

Then came the death of her son. It was the final straw. She left her two daughters with relatives in Batavia and went to Paris where she hoped to forget all her miseries.

For a brief time, Margarida danced with a vaudeville troupe. She didn't fit in with the rest of the chorus. They were coy and blond and flirtatious, but Margarida had darker skin, dark, straight hair and black, heavily lidded eyes. She looked like a panther among a litter of kittens.

Margarida decided to turn her faults into an asset. She found a new job and reappeared before the public as Mata Hari, an exotic dancer from India. She chose the name because it meant "Eye of Dawn."

"I was born," she purred, "in southern India. My family was of the sacred Brahmin caste. After my mother died, I was taught temple dances so I could take her place." Paris believed her lies.

Paris had never seen such dancing. They were accustomed to naughty, noisy can-can acts, but not the strange, exciting steps and the many layers of silks and veils that Mata Hari slowly removed from her body.

Overnight the new "Indian artist" became a sensation and the talk of France. Men courted her and begged for her love. She was given expensive clothes, furs and jewels by her admirers.

Other women in the entertainment field in Paris were quick to catch on and to copy Mata Hari. Soon there were "temple dancers" in every nightclub. Margarida was furious.

"I no longer want to see others using my ideas," she wrote to a friend. "I am leaving Paris. I will go to Berlin."

In Germany the Crown Prince first fell for her charms. He took her with him on several military trips. The Duke of Brunswick was also a close friend and admirer. Mata Hari became the toast of Germany, a jewel surrounded by men, all important men.

Later, she toured Vienna, Rome, Madrid. In each capital city she was welcomed as a great artist and followed by huge crowds.

Margarida had known as a child what it meant to be poor. She also remembered the bitterness of her marriage. Now that she was on top she wanted to live each day as richly and expensively as possible. It required much money to satisfy her appetite for luxury. Men paid a great deal to spend an evening with her.

Her German friends had the funds for her friendship. They took money set aside for spy work and presented it to her. In return they asked Mata Hari to keep her ears and eyes open, to find out what high-ranking officers in other countries knew.

Mata Hari became an agent for the master spies of Germany. History proves, however, that she was not interested in politics. Her activities were merely a way to get money for the luxuries she wanted.

During the first years of World War I, she brought attention to herself by her many trips between Paris and Berlin. She was watched, but the French and British authorities felt she was only a celebrity traveling to meet her dancing engagements.

The tip-off finally came in a wire from the Italian Secret Service:

WHILE EXAMINING PASSENGER LIST OF A JAPANESE VESSEL AT NAPLES, WE HAVE RECOG-

NIZED THE NAME OF A THEATRICAL CELEBRI-
TY, MATA HARI, THE FAMOUS HINDU DANCER.
SHE HAS, IT SEEMS, RENOUNCED HER CLAIM
TO INDIAN BIRTH AND HAS BECOME A GERMAN
CITIZEN. SHE SPEAKS GERMAN WITH A SLIGHT
EASTERN ACCENT.

Mata Hari was branded as a German spy.

French secret service men were put on her trail when she
came into France. They could find nothing except that her
letters were carried out of the country without being cen-
sored. Her many friends in the neutral governments of Holland, Sweden, and Spain were allowing her to send messages
out of France along with their diplomatic mail which was
never read by the censors.

Mata Hari's letters were taken from the Dutch and
Swedish pouches. They seemed to be harmless enough, and
no code was ever found. In spite of this, the French officials
decided to send her to Germany.

If the dancer had agreed to join her friends in Germany,
she might have never been shot. Instead, she bragged she had
many lovers there. "Let me work for the French secret service," she said. "I can get you useful information from the
enemy."

Mata Hari was sent to Brussels to spy on German General
Moritz von Bissing. She had received a list of six Belgian
intelligence officers working for France. One was executed
by the Germans a few days after her arrival. British agents
claimed the dead agent had been betrayed by a woman.

Next she was sent to Spain by way of Holland and London. In England she was delayed by Scotland Yard for ques-

tioning. "Yes," she said, "I am a spy, but I am working for France, your ally."

The Chief of Scotland Yard shook his head. "You are making a mistake. I think you should give up your spy work and go back to dancing, but if you insist, I cannot stop you."

Mata Hari took the next available boat to Spain.

There she met a number of German military attaches, including the future head of Hitler's Intelligence Service, Captain Walter Wilhelm Canaris. She again captured his fancy and was given new clothes, new jewels, and money in return for the pleasure of her company.

In Berlin, her plush days were being drawn to a close. Headquarters became aware that Mata Hari was costing too much for too little information.

Captain Canaris was ordered to get rid of the dancer-spy. He gave her a check for fifteen thousand pesetas, payable in a neutral country, and sent her to Paris to wait for another assignment for the Germans. Upon her arrival in the French capital, she was to use a coded message to tell Canaris of her safe arrival.

The "Eye of Dawn" was arrested the next day. Canaris' trap had worked well. He had given her an out-dated German code, known to the French, which linked the woman spy with the Germans beyond any doubt. So she became her own executioner.

Margarida Gertrud Zelle, the little Dutch girl who became a legendary spy, was assigned to cell No. 12 in which other women spies before her had lived: Mme. Caillaux, Mme. Stinheil and Marguerite Francillard.

On July 24, 1917, Mata Hari was brought to a trial which was held in secrecy. People thronged the streets, waiting for news of the proceedings.

Inside the courtroom, Mata Hari pleaded innocent. Her associations, she claimed, were all matters of the heart. The money, jewels and clothing came from men who loved her. Among these men, she admitted, there were Germans, but she had used them to get information for the French.

The letters? She said she had used the channels of diplomacy to get mail to her daughter. She tried to charm the court, but it did not work.

The fatal blow for Mata Hari came when she was unable to show the paper with the names of the six Belgium spies which the French secret service had given her. Nor could she find a reasonable excuse why she did not have it. Both she and the court knew the list had been sent to the German officials in Holland before she left France.

As a last resort, Mata Hari used dramatics. Facing the court, she recited a speech with gestures which she had practiced in the lonely hours in her cell:

"I count on the goodness of the hearts of you French officers. I am not French, but I am a woman who has worked for France. I have the right to have friends in other countries, even those who are at war with France. I have remained neutral."

The members of the court filed out to consider their verdict. In ten minutes they were back.

"Mata Hari is hereby sentenced to be shot as a spy!"

Margarida had been hurt before. She did not cry out. She

did not faint. She merely bit her lip and looked straight ahead.

Before her execution, Paris was filled with rumors. Some said her German lovers would ask for a pardon.

The son of a prominent French family, Pierre de Morrisac, loved her truly and plotted a mock execution. He bribed the firing squad to place blank cartridges in their guns. It was a slim chance, one that did not work.

During the time when Mata Hari was imprisoned, she was credited with far more than she ever accomplished. It was claimed she was responsible for the sinking of fourteen French transports. There was no record of such a loss. Even before her death, the seeds of her legend were beginning to sprout.

On October 15 at 5:47 Mata Hari was driven to the rifle range at Vincennes. She had written a letter to her daughter and made a final inspection of her appearance.

Witnesses waited. A procession of cars made its way to the execution spot where the guards stood on three sides of a hollow square. On the fourth side stood a bare tree, stripped of leaves and branches.

They tied her to the tree. The "Eye of Dawn" refused to have her eyes bandaged. The nuns and priest withdrew. There was the command followed by a volley of shots.

The lithe body of Mata Hari slumped, pierced by twelve bullets.

So ended the tragic, mixed-up life of one greedy Dutch girl. Mata Hari goes down in history as the first woman to be executed as a spy.

CHAPTER SIX

The Daughter of Mata Hari

When Mata Hari was shot as a spy, her daughter, Banda, was only seventeen. Banda knew very little about her mother and less about her father. Her relatives in Batavia who reared her said only her father had disappeared. "Just as well," they added. "He was worthless, a drinker and a gambler. He beat your mother. Imagine! Your mother, the toast of Europe. She will come to see you when she can, but there is a war going on. It is impossible for her to travel now."

Banda listened carefully. Her dark eyes filled with tears when she was told about her mother and father and her dead brother. In appearance Banda was much like Mata Hari but much more beautiful. Her skin was also dark, her hair straight and her eyes had a slant that made her glance attractive. While Mata Hari was tall and regal, her daughter was tiny and doll-like.

One October day in 1917, Banda received the last letter her mother ever wrote. It came from Vincennes, France, where Mata Hari was shot. This was the message:

My dear child:

There is much I would like to tell you and so little I can say. My time is getting short. It is four in the morning and within two hours I will be dead without having had the chance to see you again. You were a baby when I left you. Please believe me, I did nothing that was wrong, but war has its own cruel laws. There will be no mercy for me. No one can help. Not even my many friends.

I had a good life. At least it was a full one if not always happy. We knew so little of each other, but Aunt Rose always sent me your reports from school. She says you are intelligent and beautiful. I know you are because I have your picture.

I was young when I went to Java. I loved your father. The tropics, liquor and the death of your brother made him what he was at the last. Once he tried to kill me. I had to leave him.

Now others will kill me. I should not have gone away without you, but a better life is ahead of you without me. I will die thinking of you. You were all I had, but I did not take care of you. I have learned that money is not enough in life.

Will you pray for me? Will you think of me as a woman who wanted to do right? Life was stronger than I.

Good-bye, my child. Find your happiness in life without hating me.

Your mother,
Margarida Gertrud Zelle-MacLeod

Banda read the letter. She read the letter a second time and went to church to say a prayer for her mother, Mata Hari, who had left a trail of blood.

Banda never spoke of the last words from her mother. Few people knew her secret. She told her aunt she wanted to become a teacher, to be independent, to live away from their home.

That night she went to live with a middle-aged Dutch civil service official. He became her father, friend and teacher. Although he was forty years older than Banda, she loved him very much and asked him to marry her.

He smiled and shook his head. "No, my dear girl. I like having you with me. I enjoy spoiling you as I would a daughter, but I do not want you to have to take care of me when I am old and sick."

Following her ambition, Banda went to college and later became a teacher. She enjoyed the pioneer work of opening new schoolhouses on the islands of the Dutch colony of Java.

In 1935 Banda was shocked by the death of her old friend and protector. True to his kind and generous nature, he left her a considerable fortune. In addition, his high position in the Dutch government of the colonies had introduced Banda to many friends who came to her help during this difficult period.

All in all, her life was pleasant. She enjoyed her teaching profession and the children. Many people in Java could not read or write, and often grown men and women joined her classes and learned with their own sons and daughters.

Socially, Banda was in demand. She was beautiful, charming and well educated. Politically, her sympathies were with the Dutch, but her close association with the Oriental people gave her understanding of their way of life and problems. She was at home everywhere she went and with everybody.

So she drifted for years, happy and content.

Then ugly reality came into her life. World War II was declared in 1939, although Java was not yet involved. Her dinner parties included diplomats, spies, journalists . . . those people who wanted to know the "news behind the news."

The war moved fast. The Japanese attacked Singapore and Pearl Harbor. The British Empire seemed to crumble. The Nazis ran through Holland. The Japanese took one island after another in the Pacific, little caring whether it belonged to the French, the Dutch, the British or the United States. The islands became stepping stones for the Nipponese supply lines.

Finally, it happened. Japanese troops landed in three places on Java and swept across the country. Most of the white citizens fled but the natives remained. "Trust us," the Japanese said. "We will see that you gain your independence from Holland." The Javanese wanted to believe the invaders.

By 1942 Banda realized the sweeping tide. She often thought of her mother who had been caught in the forces of World War I. "But I will not let this happen to me," she said to herself. "Tyrants come and go, but the people remain. And after tyrants leave, there is always poverty and suffering."

She gathered her big-eyed students around her. "The world is like a big wheel," she said. "On top are the people in power who crush those beneath them. As time goes on, the wheel turns. Those who were slaves gradually get to the top and they try to crush the others."

The next day Banda was visited by a Japanese colonel. "Madame," he said bowing low and then staring into her eyes, "your recent lesson has just been brought to my attention. This is not the sort of thing the children should hear. Remember, we have come here to free the Javanese people from the Dutch. We are giving them food, money and eventually their freedom. I suggest this idea be the subject of your next lecture."

He clicked his heels and left. Banda knew he was lying.

The worried teacher went thoughtfully home. There, in her breeze-swept drawing room, was the familiar figure of her uncle whom she had not seen for ten years. Herr Paul Vanuys was Dutch, but he was wearing a Japanese uniform.

Even before tea was served Banda had the answer. Her uncle was working quite openly for the Japanese. He had turned against his own country.

"Banda, my dear," he said, "you are a popular lady in Java. People consider it an honor to attend your dinners, your parties and your dances. I want you to do a great deal more entertaining. I want you to include your own friends . . . and some we will suggest. We will pay you well."

So, that was it! Her home was to be used to get information from her friends. She was to invite Java's new masters, the Japanese, to social events that included the Dutch, the local folk and citizens of neutral nations such as Switzerland, Portugal and Sweden. It was unthinkable.

"But if I refuse to cooperate?" she said defiantly.

"I do not think you will refuse," her uncle answered. "I have an ace among the cards I hold. For instance, I could spread the interesting word that your mother was shot as a spy, a spy working for Germany. I think, my dear, that even your beauty would not save you from being marked as 'suspicious,' to say the least. And then you have said some rash things that are not complimentary to the liberators. If that were to be spread . . . I think you will find it only wise to help us."

Banda could see no way out. She agreed to do as told, but she had another plan in the back of her head.

For her there was no more quiet homelife. Her house in Batavia was filled with guests, and her servants were constantly busy. All kinds of people came: Japanese officers, the Javanese who trusted the conquerers and wanted their aid to get national independence from the Dutch, and foreign diplomats in town. Her parties went on for many months and the Japanese were greatly pleased with the results.

During this time, the Japanese decided to create a Javanese Home Guard. They knew, however, the military unit must contain no one who would revolt against Japan. Many of the leaders were selected at Banda's parties.

And during this time, love came to Banda. At one of her own dinners she was introduced to a man called Abdul. He was, her uncle said, a loyal supporter of Japan and the man who had organized the home guard. Banda shook her head sadly when she heard this. Although he was much younger than she, Abdul was so handsome and charming, it was a pity she could not share his political ideas.

It was almost as if the tall officer sensed her thoughts. He led her to the end of the veranda away from the others and smiled down into her dark eyes.

"Madam," he said, "your charm as a hostess is second only to your beauty. I hope you will let me see you often. Perhaps when there are not so many 'friends' of Java around."

There was a tone in his voice as he said "friends" that made Banda wonder. It sounded sarcastic, as if he really meant something quite different.

From that evening on, the two were together a great deal of the time. They danced at the hotel, walked through the tropical gardens, boated on the lakes . . . and fell in love. And, as lovers do, they shared their thoughts and their dreams.

Abdul confided that his position as leader of the National Guard was only a cover-up for his real activities. In reality he was one of the most important organizers of the new Indonesian underground. He was waiting for the time when the Home Guard could rise against Japan, team up with the Allies and, afterwards, establish full independence for a new United States of Indonesia. Banda joined the movement, along with hundreds of other Javanese.

Abdul decided Banda should continue her entertaining for the Japanese. She would be in the position to get much valuable information. This was what she had hoped for when she first agreed to become her uncle's hostess.

Life in Java became worse and worse. The Japanese militarists who had promised prosperity were cruel and heartless. They did not give the independence they talked of. They robbed the country of its rice, oil, rubber, quinine and copra.

In addition, they drafted Javanese labor gangs to build roads and lay tracks in the newly conquered countries of Malaya, Siam, New Guinea and Sumatra. The proud island people were slaves.

Abdul became the guide for the underground movement bent on throwing the Japanese out of his country. He held secret meetings with Gandhi and Nehru, the great Indian leaders. He had one dream: victory for the West and independence for Java.

Banda was Abdul's best agent. The daughter of Mata Hari was far more clever than her mother had ever been. She found out the Japanese plans for the battle of Guadalcanal and the amount of supplies they held. She knew the troop concentrations, airforce reinforcements and ship movements. At the same time, she helped Abdul send messengers to all the islands to enlist more and more young people for the secret Indonesian underground army.

The British and United States intelligence services had heard of Banda. They did not know she was the daughter of Mata Hari, but they knew Abdul gave the Allies the most valuable information to come from the Pacific area. And they knew Banda was his close friend.

Not until the end did the Japanese suspect Banda. She played her role of hostess cleverly and convincingly. They knew about Abdul's activities but thought it better not to arrest him. To jail Abdul would bring his followers into open revolt.

Finally the British landed. They liberated nine cities in Java, and the Japanese left one island after another as fast as they had come. The end of the terrible war was in sight. Abdul and his friends were now in command of the Home

Guard. The Indonesians were tired of foreign rulers. They had no desire to see the Dutch return, or the British stay. They publically announced the Association for a Free Indonesia. The people seized the radio station and told the world they intended to be a free nation — the United States of Indonesia.

This development was not according to Dutch plans, and it was a surprise to the British. England merely wanted to get the Japanese off the islands and to end the war, but the Dutch expected to retake Java as a colony.

Banda's parties continued. Her secret service setup seemed more effective than ever. She did not see Abdul for days at a time, but always received his orders. Her job now was to find out what the Dutch and British boundary ideas were, the Dutch occupation policy and a thousand other important facts. One of her best sources of information was a Korean, named Mato, who worked in the Dutch Governor's office. His information was always correct.

Then Banda sent Abdul her most important message. She gave the time, the place, and the plans for the Dutch attack on Indonesia.

On December 19, 1948, the Dutch army began its war against her old colony which set off one of the bloodiest conflicts in Asia. The Dutch called it a "police action" and claimed Java was not ready to rule itself nor able to keep law and order.

In the midst of the bloody confusion, Banda received another great blow in her life. Abdul, now thirty-five, announced he was going to marry another woman in the underground, a girl of twenty. Banda, almost fifty, knew she was defeated. She had lost the one man whom she really loved.

And so the fourth chapter started in Banda's life.

During the war years she had often been close to a nervous breakdown and the shock of losing Abdul put her to the final test. But, she told herself, she had duties toward Free Indonesia that could only be accomplished in the United States. If she made good, and helped to free her country, she might, in some way, make up for the selfish, sordid acts of her mother, Mata Hari. During the war years, Banda had come to realize more and more how wicked her mother had been. She was insanely anxious to make up for her acts.

So Banda went to America on a special mission. Her tiny, elegant figure, her faultless English and flawless complexion created a good impression wherever she went. She lectured on Indonesia and gave radio talks, was interviewed and toured the country in an effort to bring attention and help to her struggling nation. The new Indonesian army needed money and arms. It was Banda's job to get them.

In Hollywood Banda met a freedom-loving motion picture millionaire who promised to help. It was not without hope of a reward, however, for Banda told him that there was $750,000 in gold, hidden in her country which neither the Dutch nor the Japanese could find. He was also prodded into the venture by his fiancee, a noted film star who threatened to break her engagement if he did not cooperate.

The motion picture producer turned over large sums of money for the cause. Second-hand planes were bought and flown to Indonesia by American pilots. One plane had a special compartment to carry the gold out of the country.

The Dutch army got wind of the plan. The wild search began with the Indonesian underground moving the gold from place to place, always just one step ahead of the pursuers. Through jungles, across lakes, and over mountains the gold was carried before at last it was put on a plane, flown to the Philippines where it was transferred to neutral ownership. It was used to buy more arms for the Indonesian fight for independence—a battle which they won.

Banda returned to Indonesia in time to join the independence celebrations. She was secretly pleased with her part in the freedom movement and felt she had, in some way, made up for her mother's errors.

But her career was still not over. A messenger from the United States announced she was wanted for a special mission. The intelligence services in Washington knew of her activities and had even probed into her parentage. But her activities in the name of freedom were respected, in spite of the fact her mother had been a spy. She was sent to China to work against the Chinese Communists.

Again her reports were brilliant and accurate. She told Washington that there was no hope that Chiang Kai-shek would re-win or remain in his country. Her accounts told of Soviet supplies being pumped into Communist China. She made a place for herself in the camp of Mao Tse-tung until instructions came ordering her to go on to Korea in March, 1950. From there she reported that North Korea, backed by Soviet and Communist help, would attack South Korea. Politicians in Washington said such a move was impossible, but intelligence officers knew Banda had never been wrong.

A few months later the long, costly war started in Korea.

It was not long after this that Banda, the daughter of Mata Hari, was caught . . . by accident. The long arm of fate reached out. One of the many Communist Commissars appointed to Korea was none other than Mato, the employee of the Dutch Governor in Batavia who was once on her payroll. To be sure, Mato had worked for Indonesian freedom, but he had done so with the idea of an eventual Communist victory there . . . not merely a nationalistic success. With the failure of Communism in Indonesia, Mato was ordered back to his native Korea where he became a Commissar with the Red troops.

Mato recognized Banda, a spy for Democracy, not Communism. He turned her in to the authorities.

Banda was arrested. She was shot without trial. The time was 5:45 in the morning—the same hour her mother, Mata Hari, had been executed.

CHAPTER SEVEN

The Cat

Many people in France still remember the notices on the Paris bulletin boards, January 8, 1940: "Micheline Mathilde Carré, 40 years old, is hereby condemned to death by the Fourteenth Criminal Court."

This woman was known under the alias *La Chatte*—the Cat. She was extraordinarily beautiful, a delicate brunette with fine white teeth and marvelous eyes. The Cat was one of the greatest woman spies in Europe. Lieutenant-Colonel Achard, an officer who played a vital role in French Intelligence during the Second World War, said at her trial: "Madame Carré performed remarkable services for the French Army. During the years she worked for us, she was able to give us many of the German Army's plans of campaign."

Why then was she condemned to death by a French court?

In 1939, in a small village in southern Algeria, there lived a woman of thirty named Micheline Carré. She was married to a French Army officer. His pay was low and Micheline taught school to help out their finances.

Pretty little Madame Carré wore her brown hair in bangs over her smooth forehead. Her brown eyes looked out from under heavy well-shaped brows. She was both charming and graceful. We do not know if Micheline Carré was happy in Algeria, but the moment war broke out she decided to go to Paris.

France was calling for women for the nursing corps and Micheline joined at once. When she had her ticket and her traveling permit in her pocket, she breathed a sigh of relief. "Now," she said, "life will begin."

How do we know? Because Micheline Carré kept a diary. Each day she added to it. Her little book became a "confession," a remarkable story.

Before she left Algeria, she said goodby to her husband in Algiers. This was their last meeting, for he was killed in battle soon afterwards.

She found Algiers depressing. In her diary she wrote: "Algiers is grey, and I am nervous. I handed my suitcase to two Arabs who took me to the Hotel Terminus, where I have a room. But when I wanted a bath there was an insect running around in the tub. And later I found my floor swarming with bedbugs." While waiting for her ship to leave, Micheline walked around the suburbs, which seemed to her the only interesting parts of the city. One dark evening she rested on a bench in the picturesque Arab quarter of Algiers. A young Frenchman, dressed in the uniform of a French parachute regiment, came along and sat down beside her. In the darkness he took her for an Arab girl. Later she wrote in her diary:

"He was utterly charming, a real little bit of Paris. He was overjoyed because he was going back to France. I did not explain who I was, but talked to him as if I were an Arab girl. What charming and tender little phrases he whispered to me as we sat there! He invited me to go to a café with him. When he saw me in the lamplight and realized I was not an Arabian girl, he became frightfully confused. I was sorry I had mislead him and invited him to have breakfast with me next day. My relationship with him was charming and wonderful."

The parachute troops sailed on the ship that took Micheline to the Continent. Micheline noted in her diary: "The parachute boy was on the ship throughout the voyage."

In Paris, she moved into a hotel in the center of the city. "What a country and what a city!" she wrote. "It cannot be possible that the Nazis will conquer Paris. The historic buildings, the River Seine and its docks—Notre Dame and the Dome des Invalides. . . . I am part of these things. The boulevards are life. I walk through the streets, I sit in the café and watch the people. What sensations come to me! I am happy. I am in heaven. And I shall do my part to see that evil does not win victory over goodness."

Next day she reported for duty. During her training period in a Paris hospital, she was considered hard-working and reliable, one who cared devotedly for the wounded. When France collapsed, she was terribly shocked. Like half of France in those days, she fled from the Nazis. She set up a first-aid Red Cross station in Beauvais and then moved on to Toulouse.

Again, on her own initiative, Micheline organized a center for the wounded. She suggested to French officers that they set up a camp for men who had become separated from their units. While helping on this job she met a man who seemed to need her help more than others. He was a Polish general staff officer, helping the French Army. He had fought the Germans, been captured and escaped. Finally, wretched, starved, tired and ill, he fell into the hands of Micheline Carré. She nursed him back to health and gave him new courage.

He was called Roman Czerniawski —a name she could not pronounce. She called him "Armand" and he nicknamed her "My Cat," because of her graceful movements. Their relationship was more than a love affair. Armand outlined his plan to set up a resistance movement in France to spy on the Nazis and to fight them. The Cat willingly agreed to help.

First they had to find certain important officers of the French Army. Some were in the un-occupied zone and some were living secretly in the occupied zone. France was still in turmoil. Millions of people were moving over the roads, and the Spanish border was choked with French who were trying to escape.

The Polish colonel could not travel about freely and dared not appear in occupied France. The Cat had to do the contact work. She located and brought together the men with whom they were to work. The "Interallié" soon became the most active group in the French Resistance Movement. Colonel Marcel Achard joined it.

Achard was an important person. The other members of the group, with the exception of the Polish colonel, were all amateurs at espionage. Achard had contacts, through

Spain and Portugal, with the British. Micheline thought of him as a god.

Achard realized there was one great problem: would the Nazis remain at the Spanish border, or did they have an agreement with Generalissimo Franco to march through Spain and attack Gibraltar? Armand assigned The Cat to find out. She went to Bordeaux, then to Bayonne and Biarritz in Southern France. There, close to the Spanish-French border, a German tank unit was stationed, evidently preparing for a campaign. Air units were also being assembled in Bordeaux. Officers from these units appeared in the Cafe de Paris in Biarritz.

The Cat wrote an account of this in her diary: "A Nazi officer came in and asked, 'May I sit at your table, Madame? I need some information about the city.'

" 'Yes,' I answered, 'As a matter of fact, I'd like to ask you a question.'

" 'Please do.'

" 'You're wearing the Luftwaffe uniform and yet you don't seem to be a pilot. I don't recognize your insignia . . .'

" 'I'm what you would call in France a colonel in the quartermaster's corps. All supplies for the Luftwaffe in Bordeaux area are in my charge.' "

The officer ordered champagne and they drank together. She added in her diary: "I took care to see that I kept a clear head."

The Cat reported to Armand that the Germans were preparing to march through Spain. She stayed in the region and kept track of the German preparations. Realizing the

Nazis were slowing down, she was the first to transmit the significant news that the enemy had given up their plan to attack Gibraltar.

When her assignment was over, Micheline returned to Armand. She was completely happy. "How I love Armand! I call him my Everything, and say, 'General, at your command.' The whole world and victory over the world seem to lie in our hands. Life is like flying through the air. I have unlimited faith in him."

Colonel Achard had his group working throughout France, and The Cat worked with them. Their success was tremendous. In the British and American Intelligence Service, Achard's agents were highly respected.

The names of the most important members of the group were listed in the Allied files. The British knew about Colonel Roman Czerniawski, alias Armand; about Micheline, alias The Cat; and about other undercover workers, including the French aristocrat, Pierre de Vomecourt.

During this period the group and the British agreed on places for the air delivery of weapons for the Resistance. Naval deliveries were also assigned to safe ports along the coast. The group smuggled people over the Spanish border and into Switzerland, hid deserters from Nazis prison camps and, in general, played a game of high stakes for France.

One day Armand and The Cat decided they needed someone to help them with minor tasks, such as going into cafés and restaurants, to gather bits of information dropped carelessly by the Nazis. The Cat found such a person in Luneville. Her name was Renée Borni. Since she was going to be working closely with Armand, The Cat saw to it that this new assistant was not Armand's "type."

Renée, renamed Violette, was also an attractive woman, however, and The Cat was heart broken when she found that Armand was in love with his new agent.

In addition, The Cat had a strange feeling when she looked at Violette. There was something wrong about the woman, more than the fact that she was attractive to Armand.

In Paris, where they were staying temporarily, Micheline urged Armand to send Violette into the country, to some unimportant post. Armand smiled. "You are jealous," he teased.

"It isn't that," Micheline protested. "I have a feeling disaster is near."

"A feeling of hate, you mean," Armand laughed.

It was Renée Borni, alias Violette, who wrecked the Resistance group.

Violette had been ordered to pick up some minor facts. Near the Gare du Nord railroad station she met a German non-commissioned officer who spoke to her. She questioned him cautiously. She did not notice a man who sat behind the soldier, reading a French newspaper. She did not notice that the same man followed her when she left the café. Nor did she suspect that she was being shadowed during the next few days. Shifts of civilians took turns following her. She was seen with Armand and The Cat. Both their headquarters and their apartment were discovered. On November 18, 1941, Armand and Violette were arrested by the German "Abwehr," the Counter Intelligence Service.

A few hours later Micheline Carré was captured. The Nazi military police put her in a military prison. The quiet of her cell was maddening. She knew nothing of the others.

Had Armand been arrested too? Who else had been caught? Was she the only one of the group? With a shudder she thought of the torture awaiting her.

Night came. In her dark cell The Cat decided death was certain. She trembled as she thought of the form it would probably take. Suddenly the ceiling light was turned on. The door opened and a man in a Nazi uniform entered.

The Cat remained seated on her low stool. She gave him a frightened glance.

She recognized the man as a sergeant. In civilian clothes he would not have looked like a German. The man's actions also took her by surprise. He lingered at the door, leaning against the wall. With steady, staring eyes he watched Micheline Carré.

The Cat grew restless. She stood up. "Monsieur," she said, "why have I been arrested?" He did not answer.

After long silence he finally spoke. "You have lived in Algeria?"

"Yes, in Algeria."

"Paris is a wonderful city, isn't it?"

She stared at him in horror.

"Are you afraid?" he asked. "What are you afraid of? I'm not going to hurt you. You're an intelligent woman. Do you know that you look like Joan of Arc?"

Later she noted in her diary: "That was the most frightful part of it. The man who entered my cell was human."

This "human" person questioned her about her activities in the Resistance Movement. He talked about Algeria,

France and Paris. He spoke in a gentle voice, without accent. The Cat was amazed to realize she was having a polite, pleasant conversation with her captor.

He made a cruel joke. "It's so uncomfortable here. Shall we go somewhere else?"

Then she realized she was still in a cell. Shrugging her shoulders, she looked down at the floor. When she raised her eyes, the sergeant had vanished.

The light in the cell went out. Later she wrote: "From infinite, unreal distances I thought I heard the music of Mozart's *Requiem*. It was as if it were actually being played."

Soon a key rattled in the door. The light went on again. Armed guards stood in front of the cell. A corporal told her to follow him. Bare corridors. Bars. An office. The corporal signed a paper. A door, another door. A barred gate opening. And then . . .

Standing in the middle of an office was the sergeant who had visited her cell. But how strange he looked. He was wearing civilian clothes, elegant gloves, a silk tie and a Basque cap. He had a cigarette in his mouth and looked for all the world like an elegant Frenchman of the Boulevard des Italiens.

The gentleman in the Basque cap led her up to a large automobile and told her to get in. "In the back seat, please. And leave the curtains down."

He slid into the driver's seat. She saw the unusually large rear-view mirror at once. He could keep his eye on her. The car started, a gate opened, and she was in Paris again. The car drove into the suburbs. There was the Maison Lafitte. She could see it clearly through the windshield.

The Cat shivered with fright again. The huge palace belonged to the famous French actor, Harry Baur. The German Army had confiscated the building and was using it as their counterespionage headquarters. If she was being taken here, they knew everything. No unimportant spies were brought to this house.

Once inside Micheline was more confused than ever. It was not like the center of German Counter-intelligence—the polite servants, the elegant drawing room. And she was left alone.

The Cat sat in a comfortable chair and stared out of the window into the dark park. From far away came the noises of the great city. No one seemed to notice her.

Suddenly the door opened. The man who had driven the car asked her to come along. He led the way down the hall to a living room with luxurious furniture. She looked through a doorway and saw a mirror, with a lighted lamp in front of it. The room was a bedroom.

What happened that night?

Her diary does not say. Later the French court tried to find out. The presiding judge asked: "Tell the story exactly as it happened. You went to Harry Baur's villa?"

"I've told it exactly as it happened," she answered, "but I'll tell it again. After fourteen months of struggle and ceaseless work for the Resistance Movement, I was arrested and taken to Harry Baur's villa, the Maison Lafitte. I was in the power of the Nazis. Sergeant Hugo Bleicher did not leave me alone for a moment."

"Then you found out the name of this sergeant?"

"He called himself Hugo Bleicher."

"Was his military rank really that of a sergeant?"

"I don't know."

"Was his real name Hugo Bleicher?"

"How could I possibly know, your honor?"

"All right. You were Bleicher's prisoner. Did you let him make love to you that first night?"

"Can't you put yourself in my place, your honor?"

"Answer my question."

"Must I really tell you all about it, your honor?"

"Yes."

"Bleicher said to me, 'If you are nice to me, you'll be free tonight.' "

"Didn't it shock you—you, the widow of a French Army officer—to be 'nice' to a Nazi sergeant?"

"Very well, your honor, it shocked me."

"What else happened that night?"

Silence.

"I want to know what else happened that night."

Silence.

"We all want to know what happened. That is what you must explain. For fourteen months you were in great danger working for your resistance group. And after one single night you forgot your whole past, forgot France and yourself. Eight hours after that night you turned over to this

Sergeant Hugo Bleicher the thirty-five most important fighters in the French Resistance Movement. Now what happened that night?"

The Judge stared at The Cat for a full minute.

The morning after "that night," The Cat and Hugo Bleicher, wearing civilian clothes, got into a small car with French number plates. They drove into Paris and stopped at the house where some members of the Resistance were hiding. No one noticed when several more cars driven by civilians also parked at the curb. One man got out and bought a newspaper. Another bought cigarettes.

The Cat went upstairs and knocked on a door, using a signal. The door was opened at once. Rocchini and Frank were there, both prominent members of the group. They were surprised when they saw the unknown man at The Cat's side.

"Something must be done," The Cat whispered. "Armand has been arrested."

The two men gasped.

"Don't worry about him," she said, pointing to Bleicher. "You don't know him, but he is one of us."

They talked about Armand for several minutes. Then The Cat said to Bleicher, "Go downstairs and start the car. We must waste no time."

After Bleicher left there came another knock at the door. Micheline opened it. Nazis with drawn revolvers shouted, "Hands up!"

This became the standard plan. During the next eight

hours it was used again and again, until thirty-five leaders of the French Resistance had been arrested.

For two months The Cat followed all of Bleicher's orders. She knew everything, and she betrayed everything she knew. Many of her fellow-resisters were sent to prison. But the man Bleicher wanted most was Colonel Achard.

But The Cat never betrayed Achard. The Colonel testified in court: "She knew where I was hiding, but she did not tell."

The Cat made excuses to Bleicher. She said she didn't know where Achard was, and he believed her. She offered to find another very important man, Pierre de Vomecourt. Bleicher was excited when he heard the name. Then he grew thoughtful. He recognized there were even greater possibilities than to arrest Pierre de Vomecourt.

The Cat was sent back to her old headquarters. Bleicher's plan had been flawless. The captured men had had no time to give warning. The Resistance did not know of the plot and accepted their Cat with open arms.

For the next two months The Cat again worked with the French. No one had the slightest suspicion of her. None of the men and women in the Resistance Movement dreamed that their trusted and courageous comrade, Micheline Carré, was a traitor. She reorganized the group work and inspired everyone with new courage.

But every night The Cat was secretly driven to Villa Baur. There she told the French plans made during the day. She reported that the main worry of the people in the Resistance was how to keep a contact with England. All the French go-between men had been arrested.

When Bleicher heard this, he ordered The Cat to ask Pierre de Vomecourt to come to Paris. He explained to her that Vomecourt would have to be sent to England for the Resistance Movement. She must persuade her comrades that Vomecourt was the most capable person to go.

The following night Bleicher told The Cat he had a surprise for her. "When you get home you'll find Violette there. She's never really been arrested, of course, because she's working for us. Violette will keep her mouth shut. Take care of her. Her assignment is to stay in the Resistance Movement."

The Cat carried out all her orders. In "Pam-Pam," a café on the Champs Elysees, she met Pierre de Vomecourt. She made her proposal, and he, a serious and sincere patriot, agreed. They would try to get to England. Once there he would inform their British friends what had been happening, and obtain help.

The trip, Micheline pointed out, was a difficult one. The secret paths across the border into Spain had been discovered by the Nazis. They also knew the places on the coast where Resistance members were taken out to sea and shipped to England. But she would try to find a way.

A few days after this "Pam-Pam" conversation, The Cat saw her Resistance friends again. She said she had found a way to get to England. She explained that she would have to go along with Pierre de Vomecourt because she could help him make the trip safely.

The others agreed. This was their clever Cat, the heroine of the Resistance. They thought she deserved her fame. She was the smartest, the best of them all, and the bravest.

Bleicher saw to it that The Cat and Pierre got out of France safely. Bleicher did even more. He arranged for The Cat and victimized Pierre de Vomecourt to secure jobs in the War Office in London.

For nine months The Cat worked there. She sent all her information through the routes the Resistance Movement had set up. Her messages went to Violette, and Violette reported to Bleicher.

But then came the black day in The Cat's life. Pierre, the British Counter-Intelligence Service and Scotland Yard had unmasked her. In July, 1942, The Cat was arrested. The British kept her in prison until the end of the war.

While in prison she wrote in her diary a paragraph addressed to her former comrades in the French Resistance: "Oh, how much I have endured. Never shall I be able to find words to express my deep and endless sorrow, or to describe my fears. But I am not alone. You, too, those of you who are still living, will not fall asleep tonight; you will be with me. You, the dead, and I—we will live by our own laws in a world I have found for myself."

In January, 1949, she stood calmly before the French judges.

The prosecutor spoke: "For two months she practiced the worst kind of treason. Her diary, from which I have read you parts, describes her as what she is: a brain without a heart—you will have to judge all this. And you will recognize that there is only one possible penalty: Death."

The defense attorney answered: "I admit her guilt. But you must consider that this woman was faced with the choice of life or death. Do not forget that from the beginning of the Resistance she was a heroine. Would you put to death those who at the beginning sowed the seed of faith and later over-estimated their own strength?"

But before sentence was pronounced The Cat lost control of herself. She cried out to the court: "I await the verdict without fear. But I can't help remembering that while the death sentence is being asked for me in this court, Hugo Bleicher is living free in . . . Hamburg!"

"Condemned to death"—was the verdict of the court.

A few months later the President of the Republic of France commuted Micheline Carré's sentence to life imprisonment.

CHAPTER EIGHT

Allan in Wonderland

Among the files of the New York Police are the notes on "Allan Johnson." From them it is possible to find the thread of an astonishing, almost unbelievable story.

It began when Allan Johnson, a young engineering student, left his parents' home after a long week-end in New York to return to college. After the usual traffic delays he arrived at Grand Central Station to find his train had pulled out just a few seconds before.

He was furious. He would have to miss classes on the following day. He stood there, a forlorn figure in Grand Central Station, counting his money to make certain he could afford to go to a theatre. Suddenly a girl walked up to him and whispered, "I told you butter wouldn't suit the works."

Allan stood there dumbfounded and stared at the young woman. Was she drunk, crazy, or trying to get his attention? Allan knew his classic literature, particularly Lewis Carroll's *Alice in Wonderland*. He responded by quoting the

March Hare's reply to the same remark at the Mad Hatter's Tea Party. "It was the *best* butter."

The young woman seemed satisfied with Allan's reply and whispered, "Seven o'clock sharp, 890 East Seventh Street."

Then she looked at the huge Grand Central Station clock and exclaimed, "You are seven minutes early. Next time you better be on time."

With that angry reminder she quickly disappeared among the milling crowd. Allan was astonished. Was he involved in some dark mystery? Could it be that this unknown girl was the messenger of some gangsters or killers?

He wrote down the address the girl had given him and stood pondering. His first thought was to wait and see what would happen next. He moved away a few yards, bought a newspaper, and from behind it watched the spot where he had stood, just under the station clock. At precisely three o'clock a young man wearing a brown suit arrived and took a position there. The man took out his wallet, counted the money in it and watched the clock.

Then Allan, hardly knowing why, threw away his newspaper, walked over to the young man and said, "I told you butter wouldn't suit the works."

"It was the *best* butter!" the young man repeated in a foreign accent.

To this Allan was prompted to reply, "Get out of town. They're wise to us!"

Like a guest at Macbeth's feast, the mysterious young man did not wait. With a frightened glance at Allen, he dashed out of sight.

It didn't take Allan Johnson long to find the nearest police station, where he told his story to the desk-sergeant. The sergeant asked Allan a few questions and then commented that the giant city of New York was filled with cranks and crackpots. Allan's story was certainly interesting, but where would they find this woman and the man he had described in a city of eight and a half million people? It was impossible.

Allan was insistent, and rather than argue, the sergeant wrote up the details. But they were far too thin. Finally the sergeant said, "Look, don't waste your short time in New York, and don't waste ours . . . Goodby."

But Allan refused to go. In order to get rid of him the sergeant sent him to the lieutenant at precinct headquarters. At the precinct Allen retold his strange story. Lieutenant O'Connor laughed and said that Allan, as a college student, ought to know that quoting famous literature was not illegal. Anyway there was not a chance in a million of finding the two people.

"Go home," was all Lieutenant O'Connor had to say.

But Allan was stubborn. At last the police lieutenant agreed to send him in a police car to the address the woman had given. If they came across anything suspicious, an investigation could be made.

Patrolman Short accompanied Allan in the squad car. Again Allan told his story. The patrolman was impressed and told the young student he might have stumbled onto some kind of racket—dope peddling or smuggling. Allan was excited. There was the scent of adventure in the air.

The patrol car pulled into Seventh Street, a one-way street. It was a busy but depressing neighborhood. Patrolman Short, after a quick glance around, said, "There is no such number in the street as 890. But a second search showed there was such a building. It was a dark, empty shell. The roof and windows were gone, and the floors had been ripped up. The neighboring house, 892, looked as ghostly.

Short told Allan to stay in the car while he questioned the foreman of the demolition squad. When he returned he told Allan the men had been working there for two weeks. A new parking lot was to be built on the site. There was evidently nothing shady going on at the address.

Allan was crestfallen when the bottom fell out of his great mystery. He felt he had made a fool of himself. He asked Short to drop him off on Broadway so that he could go to a movie. "Let's forget about the whole thing," he said, "I'm sorry."

The movie did not take Allan's mind off the past events. There must be more to it, he thought. He took out the envelope on which he had written the address and by the light of the screen read it once more. No, there had been no mistake. It was the right address.

Suddenly the truth flashed across his mind. Why hadn't he thought of it before? He remembered the girl had told him to be at 890 East Seventh Street at seven o'clock. She did not ask him to be inside. Had he waited outside perhaps the mystery would have been solved. He glanced at his watch. It was six o'clock. Should he first phone the lieutenant? He thought it over and decided he would do his own investigating.

Allan hailed a taxi and went to Seventh Street, paid the driver and walked toward the East River. The street was deserted and dimly lighted. It was now 6:45. He leaned against a lamppost and waited.

Minutes passed. Then he saw a man walking slowly toward the house. The stranger was well-dressed and wore glasses. He used a cane to feel his way. The man stopped in front of Allan.

"Seven maids," he said.

Again Allan remembered *Alice* and answered, "Seven mops."

"Follow me," said the blind man. He walked on, tapping with his cane.

As they walked east along Seventh Street, the old rhyme echoed through Allan's mind:

> "If seven maids with seven mops
>   Swept for half a year,
>   Do you suppose," the Walrus said,
> "That they could get it clear?"
> "I doubt it," said the Carpenter,
>   And shed a bitter tear.

The man finally came to a halt and took Allan's arm. They had stopped at the eleventh house in the block, and, still gripping Allan, the blind man groped his way down the steps to the cellar entrance. It was pitch black as he fumbled in his pocket for the key to open the door. Inside, it was just as dark. They walked along the corridor to a second door. Allan's unknown companion knocked three times. There were voices inside, and then the door was flung open. The strong light from two naked bulbs almost blinded Allan, but when he was able, he studied the men in the room. One was a giant, as big and hairy as King Kong, the gorilla. Behind him, in an easy chair and facing the door, was a swarthy individual, evidently the one who gave the orders.

The blind man threw his cane on the table and guided Allan to a nearby chair. The boss and the blind man conversed in English, but with a European accent. The boss turned to Allan.

"We have no time to lose," he said. "They will leave their hotel at 8 o'clock. They are very punctual as you know. This is Paul, your driver." He pointed to the giant. "You will sit in front with Paul. The gun is in the car. Nino will be behind you in case anything should go wrong. They will probably come out together. In that case you will have to kill both of them. If Androsow should come first, let him pass. Berenkow is more important, for reasons which need not concern you. If he comes out first, let him have it and forget about Androsow. You understand my orders?"

Allan held onto the sides of his chair. He understood only too well that he was being briefed for his role in a political assassination that was to take place that very night. Berenkow was the Ukrainian delegate to the United Nations, Androsow, Deputy Foreign Minister of the Soviet Union. The harsh voice of the man in the chair interrupted Allan's thoughts.

"Your car will develop engine trouble just south of the main entrance. Paul will raise the hood and pretend to examine the engine. At this spot you will have a clear line of fire. I am given to understand that you never miss. However, let me warn you that should you fail, or lose your nerve, or try to change your mind at the last minute, Nino has orders to kill you instantly."

Having stood silently by while the boss explained the scheme, Paul took up his gun, and the blind man handed an envelope to Allan containing five hundred dollars. The rest, he was told, would be paid after it was all over. Later, Allan admitted to the police that he was close to breaking down and confessing that he was only a young engineering student, not an assassin and spy. But had he done so, he would never have gotten out of the house alive.

Paul and Nino led Allan to the car outside. The driver handed him the gun for the assassination. Not a word was exchanged. Allan knew he was in a spot and hadn't a notion how to get out of it. Nino sat behind him in the car as it moved uptown to the west side, then turned east to the entrance of the Waldorf Astoria Hotel, headquarters of the Soviet delegation to the United Nations.

Still no word had passed between the men. Paul was an excellent driver. Time and again he slipped out of traffic jams until he reached the appointed spot right on time. Paul slipped out of the car and lifted the hood. At that moment the Russians came out of the building. Nino growled, "Shoot fast." Allan felt the gun in his hand. It was an awful moment. Luckily for him he was never called upon to make his decision. The men heard a warning shriek as a car crashed into their own. Paul and Nino were thrown forward, and Allan went through the window into the street—and into blackness.

It was not until many hours later that he regained consciousness. When he came back to life he had no idea where he was. Gradually, he saw the white bed and knew he was in a hospital. "I'm dying," he murmured. Then he saw Lieutenant O'Connor at his bedside.

"No, you're alive," O'Connor said with a grin. "You have a rather bad concussion, but you'll get over it. But you were very, very lucky."

O'Connor told him the rest of the story. "I couldn't figure out what you were going to do. Then I knew I had to bump hard, very hard, to make sure it would not happen."

Allan smiled weakly. "So you were around all the time!"

"The big one is dead," O'Connor continued, "and the smaller man is much worse off than you are."

"You mean the Soviet delegates were killed?"

"Oh, no," laughed O'Connor. "We didn't take any chances with you. We followed after you left us, and we were at the movies with you. Six men were on the job."

"The blind man, what happened to him?" asked Allan.

"A squad car picked him up. We think we have every member of the gang," the lieutenant answered.

Allan closed his eyes and sighed contentedly. What a busy Sunday night it had been!

Thus ends the story of a plot to assassinate the Kremlin delegates to a United Nations conference in New York. The facts were never made public, and the intended victims were never aware how much they owed to a young engineering student with a questioning mind.

CHAPTER NINE

Ruth, Behind the Attack on Pearl Harbor

Modern crazes had hit the Hawaiian Islands. Juke boxes and swing music drowned out the native music sung by the tanned Polynesian girls. And there was a brand new topic for conversation in Honolulu.

The islands of Oahu could now boast an ultra-modern beauty parlor! Ruth, the store's manager, was well liked. She gave excellent permanents and was skillful with dyes and rinses. She installed elegant equipment and brought in a staff whose skill at hair-do's and facials compared favorably with the treatments of New York's Fifth Avenue.

The beauty salon, highly fashionable, soon became the clearing house for local gossip. Women discussed who was in town, who was leaving, furloughs, assignments, ship arrivals and departures. This was the chit-chat that made up the life of the islands and naturally could not be kept out of usual conversation.

The beauty parlor opened in 1939. Nobody on the Hawaiian islands thought of war, and few back in the mother country dreamed it would come. But espionage is a continuout business, pursued in peace times as well as during war.

This particular plot did not begin in the German War Office. The hand of Admiral Walter Wilhelm Canaris, Nazi Germany's spy chief, was not in it. All the credit is due to Propaganda Minister Joseph Goebbels, who committed suicide in 1945.

Goebbels had held office for two years when, in the beginning of 1935, he gave a party at the Ministry for all the personnel. It was a gala affair, with everyone feeling happy and proud, inspired by the newborn strength of Nazi Germany. Goebbels, who never denied his interest in women, was in his element. This evening promised the beginning of a new romance for him.

His private secretary, Leopold Kuehn, was at the party with his young sister, Ruth. The girl was beautiful. Goebbels danced with her the whole evening. Ruth realized that to have the Propaganda Minister as an admirer was an important thing. She saw him often after that night of champagne and dancing.

However, Frau Goebbels thought differently. She watched the two until she could stand it no longer and then firmly ordered Ruth out of Germany. The Propaganda Minister, however, knew he would have to place Ruth and her family far away where they would be happy and there would be no scandal.

One of Goebbels' closest friends was Dr. Karl Haushofer, son of the famous general and geopolitician. If Goebbels wanted anything in Haushofer's power to grant, there was no further question about it.

Yes, Haushofer could use the young lady, Ruth Kuehn. The old general, who had visited Japan and seen the possibilities there as early as 1914, was in regular contact with that country. Very recently his Japanese associates had expressed a need for white men and women.

Japan's government, through Haushofer, wanted white folk to help in the Japanese spy service and in the Kempeital, Japan's secret military police force. Japan, in fact, needed a good many people for intelligence work. Haushofter therefore informed Goebbels that he had openings not only for Ruth Kuehn, but for her brothers and parents, provided they were intelligent and careful and had received a course of basic training.

It is not only theatrical blood that can run through a family. In this case the entire family was involved, and all had a talent for, spying, although Ruth seemed to be the smartest. Her family background was also helpful.

Ruth's father, Dr. Bernard Julius Otto Kuehn, was born in Berlin. He was forty, and Ruth eighteen. When the doctor was eighteen he had enlisted in the German Navy and served as a midshipman aboard a cruiser in the first World War. When the ship was sunk in a battle with a British battleship in 1915, he was taken prisoner and landed in England, where he quickly learned English. When the armistice came, he was still a young man and decided to take up medicine. Very early he accepted Nazi thinking. He also filled Ruth with the ideas of the monster, Adolf Hitler. Unable to make the grade as a doctor, Kuehn accepted a position in the Gestapo under Heinrich Himmler, a personal friend. Long afterward, Dr. Kuehn complained that the Gestapo had promised a good job as police chief in one of the German cities. Instead, through

the romance of his beautiful but reckless daughter, he was
exiled to Hawaii.

When the Kuehn family landed in the Hawaiian Islands
on August 15, 1935, they were not the usual run of pleasure-
seeking tourists. The father was a scientist, a trim, grey-haired
professor. They were all well bred and handsome people.
Doctor Bernard Julius Otto Kuehn came with his family, except his son Leopold, who remained in Berlin as Goebbels'
secretary. With him were Frau Professor Friedel Kuehn, his
six-year-old son, Hans Joachim, and his daughter, Ruth.

A well-knit family, their domestic life was a joy to behold.
They said in Hawaii the father was interested in the Japanese
language. The doctor and his daughter were also very much
interested in the ancient history of the islands. They traveled
around, visiting the old lava temples of the early Polynesians.
Very soon they knew the islands as well as the back of their
hands. Ruth loved the seashore and surfing, as did the whole
family. They swam often, or they would hire a boat and go
exploring. Friedel, the mother, was a commonplace sort of
matron, but extremely helpful. She listened and observed details of military significance when she only appeared to be a
housewife. Twice during the period 1936-1941 she traveled
as a messenger to Japan, but neither the F.B.I. nor the U.S.
Navy Intelligence suspected her.

Ruth, slim and tall, worked according to plan. She made
great headway with her English. She was a wonderful dancer
and attended every important social affair. She attracted
scores of naval officers who were more handsome than her
club-footed ex-lover, Dr. Goebbels.

When asked, the Kuehns would answer that they did not
like the Nazis. Ruth always added, "I was so young when we

left Germany." Neighbors and acquaintances had the impression that the Kuehns were very well off. They had a beautiful home, beautiful art pieces, exquisite silver, all the signs of a family of culture and wealth.

During the first three years on the islands, the Kuehns received seventy thousand dollars, transmitted through a Honolulu bank by the Rotterdam Bank Association. On one of her trips, Friedel returned from Japan with sixteen thousand dollars in cash.

The F.B.I. and American Army and Navy Intelligence have since learned that during this period the family received over one hundred thousand dollars. There was probably more which has not been traced.

Considering the great expenses, espionage is less well paid than is commonly thought, but the Kuehns received more than their fair share. Intelligence work is often limited to the reporting of gossip, research, information gleaned from naval and merchant marine men. Ruth knew how to handle men. And Ruth was clever, glamorous and desirable. Her step-father encouraged her to meet the officers, the more the merrier. With war drawing near, more and more was demanded of them.

The Kuehns were in the service of two countries. Though General Haushofer had lent them to the Japanese, the Nazis soon discovered their value. Copies of all reports went to Germany. The Kuehns thought it only fair to ask for more money. Besides, Ruth's appetite for expensive things had grown. So had the doctor's.

Early in 1939, Dr. Kuehn decided he needed a quiet place to get on with his study of the Japanese language. He moved his family from Honolulu to Pearl Harbor. The Japanese

Secret Service plan, for which Ruth and the doctor had been sent to the Islands, began to take shape.

Ruth established herself as a popular favorite among the young people and the wives of the Navy men. She let it be known that she had a flair for the art of personal grooming. In 1939, she announced the opening of a beauty parlor, and the enterprise was greeted with enthusiasm. Even Ruth was not prepared for its great success. Friedel, too, began to spend much of her time at the new salon. Both reported daily to the doctor what they had picked up. Couriers of the German and Japanese consulates relayed the information to their own countries.

Then one day the Japanese Vice-Consul at Honolulu, smart little Otojiro Okuda, sent for Ruth and her father. They together, met secretly. Okuda told them the time had come to get hold of some real maritime information—exact dates, locations, figures on the U.S. Naval forces in the Pacific. He complimented them on their past work, but this job, he emphasized, was of another order. The Japanese would be willing to pay generously, and it would mean a deadly blow against the United States Navy.

Ruth asked forty thousand dollars but her father agreed to take fourteen thousand as an advance, the rest to be paid when the job was done.

Father Kuehn was worried. Where could he get the information? Ruth laughed. The next day she announced her engagement to one of the highest U.S. Naval officers stationed in Pearl Harbor. She was in control now, and her stepfather had to work for her. Still, he was good at research. Together they made a perfect team. Ruth gave him new orders and shortly after their conversation with Okuda, Dr. Kuehn began to stroll daily along the fortified sections of Pearl Harbor. "Take Hans Joachim along," she ordered.

Hans Joachim, now ten, was a great help. The father explained the waterfront scene to the child, who was "just crazy about" every aspect of the American Navy. After a while the American sailors invited the boy on board a battleship and pointed out the wonders of this giant toy. Dr. Kuehn, an alien, was never permitted aboard, and he was far too clever to expect an invitation. He allowed the boy to go alone.

The same night, Ruth met the officers of the same battleship, and next morning reported for son, daughter and father. The report was transmitted to Tokyo and Berlin. Washington hadn't the slightest notion of these messages.

Success pushed them on. Ruth sent her father to inform Japanese Consul Okuda that they had worked out a signal system designed to transmit information on the number and kinds of American ships in Pearl Harbor, the fleet's exact location, and ship movements in general. The Consul agreed the plan would work for signaling to the Japanese fleet and air force.

The Kuehns owned a second home, a small house in Kalama, on the lee side of Oahu. Ruth spent a lot of time at their week-end place. She had bought a pair of eighteen-power binoculars, a purchase that might have been considered unusual for a young lady.

The light signals were to be flashed from the window of their Kalama home. Ruth, her father, Consul Okuda and the fourth secretary of the Japanese Consulate, Tadesi Morimura, worked out a practical code. On December 2, 1941, daughter and father tried out their new system for the first time. It worked. On the same day, Vice-Consul Okuda received a written tabulation of the number, types and exact location of American ships in Hawaiian waters. The night before, Ruth had come in after a very late date with her fiance. He said later that they had talked about the ships in harbor for several hours.

Next morning Japanese Consul-General Nagoa Kita, Okuda's superior, transmitted all data via short wave to the Japanese Naval Intelligence office.

All was now in readiness for the "Day of Infamy," the Japanese attack on Pearl Harbor. Ruth and her father knew the exact day of the attack . . . the exact hour.

On December 7, 1941, Ruth Kuehn opened the window, and her father gave the light signals. He told the Japanese what to bomb and what not to bomb. He directed them to the most important points. Dr. Kuehn used the flashlight while Ruth gave the messages. The two led the attack on Pearl Harbor from that one window.

Zooming overhead, the Japanese bombers spread ruin among the American fleet. One third was sunk or severely damaged. Everything proceeded according to the Kita-Okuda-Kuehn plan—or almost.

Rarely is there a perfect crime. This one was no exception. In one respect their plan went wrong. The Japanese Consul had arranged to have a Jap submarine pick him and the Kuehn family up and take them to Tokyo. The Kuehns planned to move quickly. They would leave even their toothbrushes behind, taking only money, crisp paper dollars. Ruth insisted each should carry and keep a part of the total amount. Once in Japan they would share the balance of twenty-six thousand dollars due to them.

But amid the noise and fire of Pearl Harbor, U.S. Intelligence officers spotted the lights coming from the window of the Kuehn house. Before the Japanese submarine arrived, Kuehn and his family were picked up by the authorities. Ruth and Friedel protested. The doctor refused to answer questions. But all the facts were against them. An outline of the signal system was found. And there was far too much money in the house, some of it in Japanese currency. The women were filling money belts and bags when the police arrived. The binoculars came to light, and copies of reports written in German.

Dr. Kuehn finally admitted everything. He did his best, though, to protect Ruth and his wife. He insisted that he alone was responsible. Ruth declared she was in charge and said her father only obeyed her orders. Friedel claimed she had bought the binoculars and was the leader of the gang.

On February 21, 1942, Dr. Kuehn was sentenced to be shot. He knew he was fighting for his life. He became frightened. Ruth's trial was coming up. He had to save her. He tried to bargain, to make a deal with Uncle Sam. For years he had been in the service of the Germans and Japanese, and now he offered his services to the Americans. United States officials told him he couldn't buy his or his daughter's pardon that way.

The death sentence was signed. Kuehn found his lonely cell a madhouse. Ruth seemed to be calm, waiting. She had always been able to find a way out.

Dr. Kuehn finally begged for mercy. He promised to tell U.S. Navy Intelligence all he knew about enemy espionage in the Pacific. He claimed he was the master spy who had organized the network. Ruth was innocent; his wife, a harmless homemaker. U.S. Intelligence officers made no promises but told him to confess all—and he did. Dr. Kuehn's sentence was changed on October 26, 1942 to thirty years' hard labor in Alcatraz prison, on an island in San Francisco Bay. Ruth and Friedel were held and are now free in Germany. Leopold Kuehn, the son who had remained with Goebbels, shared the downfall of his family in another way: he died in Russia. Friedel later tried, unsuccessfully, to commit suicide.

Another of Friedel's daughters lives under an assumed name in Los Angeles. She told me part of this story.

CHAPTER TEN

The American Powder
Puff Commandos

In the minds of many people the underworld of espionage, outside of fiction, is commanded entirely by men. But the United States employed around one thousand women intelligence agents during the war years, 1941-1945. Not all of these worked for the Central Intelligence Agency. Many were enrolled in far more dangerous activities for the Office of Strategic Services, the OSS.

I remember a charming nineteen-year-old girl who, single-handed, was responsible for the destruction of a Nazi oil refinery because of her Sherlock Holmes ability to put X and X together and get the right answer.

She was hired as a research secretary, but she had a quick brain, a sense of humor and a desire to follow her "hunches."

Erma spoke German fluently and was given the job of screening applicants for intelligence work against the Nazis during World War II. One of the tests involved figuring out freight rates from a German schedule and timetable to show the applicant's knowledge of the German language, measures, currency, and so forth.

While giving one of these tests, Erma became fascinated by a small item in the freight rates. The more she studied it, the more excited she became. She could hardly wait for the testee to complete his work before she dashed to the office of her superior officer.

"Sir," she said, "there is something strange here." She handed him the schedule.

The colonel glanced down the list of figures and then looked up at her.

"What do you find so unusual about this?"

"If you will permit me, sir," said Erma, passing around to the side of the desk and pointing to some items at the bottom of the page. "These tables give rates on oil shipments to some small village in Austria."

"Well?"

"This village never had a railroad before . . . and Austria has little oil. Now, why in the world should Nazis ship oil to that God-forsaken town near the Hungarian border unless there is a new refinery that we don't know about?"

The colonel thought for a moment. "That's an interesting theory, and one we should look into. Thank you for drawing my attention to these figures. You may have found something of value to us."

As Erma left the office, she could hear the officer snapping on the buttons of the inter-com system.

Reconnaissance planes were sent over Austria. The photographers brought back pictures of a cleverly camouflaged refinery near the Austrian-Hungarian border.

Twenty-four hours later U.S. Air Force bombers paid the area a visit and left the refinery in ruins.

Mission accomplished because of a clever woman.

Another, Rachel Geise, member of the OSS, appeared to be a hard-working professor at New York's Columbia University. But conducting her classes was secondary to a most difficult, and in many ways, remote task . . . that of gathering, controlling and compiling all incoming information from North Africa. She pieced these facts together to get a clear intelligence picture of the Nazi and Petain organization in North Africa. Under her guidance, spy rings were set up in Algeria. Agents from Africa, France and Italy were pumped for information that later was valuable during the invasion of North Africa.

The woman professor was called upon again to prepare intelligence reports needed for the invasion of southern France. On Marseilles alone, her report included the names and addresses of the owners of thirty-two cafes and a list of suspicious customers who went there often.

Her rewards for the Marseilles report was the Legion of Merit medal and the satisfaction that she had helped her country.

While Dr. Geise was taking various trips to North Africa to set up her agents, there was another woman who operated on the theory that New York, the eastern gateway in the United States to the world, was also a great source of information. There was, she contended, not one military secret that could not be uncovered in that giant city.

Mrs. Emmy Rado, a soft-spoken middle-aged woman, had the job of interviewing refugees, foreigners and naturalized citizens. Although she used other pretenses, her objective was to obtain needed information about Europe and North Africa.

One of her assignments was to secure all available data on harbors and military defenses of Bone, Algeria, the proposed invasion spot for the Allied armies.

After a long search through newcomers to New York, Mrs. Rado unearthed a refugee who had lived in Bone.

"What was your profession in Algeria?" she asked the Algerian.

"I was a hydraulic engineer," he replied.

Knowing that she must be cautious in order to avoid raising suspicions, Mrs. Rado threw out a feeler.

"I'm writing a textbook for college students on the economic life of colonial nations. I would be happy to pay you for any material you can give me on Algeria. After all," and she laughed, "you have lived there. Who am I to write about your country?"

The refugee smiled back. "Mrs. Rado, I would be happy to help you. I want people to know about my country, and I can also use the money."

During the following weeks the two spent many hours together. A secretary took down what appeared to be harmless notes about the way of life of the Algerian people, their problems, facts and statistics. But out of the mass of information, the OSS obtained what it wanted: details about oil pipelines, water depths in the harbor, fortification locations, ammunition depots, troop placements, general and specific defenses.

The U.S. Army is slow to give praise, but later Mrs. Rado was told the notes for the "textbook" were one of the great scoops of the war.

While the researchers have been the most important people in the spy field and have included such people as Erma, Professor Geise and Mrs. Rado, their behind-the-scene activities are not as glamorous as those of the more active women in the trade. Many adventurous charmers have known action, sometimes torture and death.

There was Artemis. Her real name can never be mentioned. Carrying a forged passport with her code name, she was landed secretly by submarine in Normandy, made her way through France by cart, train, on foot into the Haute-Loire territory. There she found work until she could build up her position as a liaison officer with the French resistance movement. In the weeks before she landed on the cold coastline of France, Artemis had been briefed by General de Gaulle in London. Her job was the gigantic task of organizing the scattered members of three groups of the French underground into demolition squads.

Artemis was neither beautiful nor was she ugly. She was neither young nor old, but she was clever and forceful. She met her "students" in barns and in peasant kitchens, in the forests and in back rooms. There she gave lessons in the art of demolition . . . a stick of dynamite should be placed "thus so" under a railroad track, a wire set to a fuse "thus so" in an automobile.

Her followers learned rapidly and enthusiastically. They also branched out and established an effective network of underground radio stations.

In one act of sabotage, Artemis, alone and unaided, showed her skill by blowing up a bridge while a German convoy of trucks was passing over it. It was estimated that a hundred Nazi soldiers were killed in the explosion.

For unflinching bravery the most unforgettable character of the last war was a woman from the "Wild West." Dubbed "High Pockets," a name which came from the waist-high pockets of the cowboys, this woman swore revenge when her husband was killed by the Japanese.

For over three years she spied on Japanese troop movements in the Philippines and reported directly to General MacArthur. In her "spare" time she smuggled food to the starving United States prisoners of war in the death camps. In many cases she sacrificed her own personal feelings and was friendly with Japanese camp officials and guards.

Two out of three spies were caught in the last war. High Pockets was among them. She was not so fortunate as to be executed.

The Japanese slowly removed fingernail by fingernail, toenail by toenail, in an effort to make her repent and, more than that, to make her talk. When the water treatment failed, they left her to die.

It is a miracle, but High Pockets survived. At the end of the war she was decorated by the President of the United States.

The late conductor, Arturo Toscanini, one of the greatest orchestra conductors of our time, must have had many thoughts in his mind as he rapped his baton, calling for silence before the beginning of Beethoven's Fifth Symphony, the musical trademark of the Allies in World War II.

His own daughter, Mrs. Wally Castelbaro, worked as a spy for the Office of Strategic Services.

Through her family ties, Mrs. Castelbaro was in the position of knowing the wise thing to do.

She lived, worked and fought with the Italian underground groups: "Once," she says, "we shot it out with a German army unit at a range of sixty yards."

The conductor's daughter held many secret conferences in obscure places. She traveled through the Nazi lines to keep her appointments.

A large part of her journey had to be made on foot. Finally she reached the border of Switzerland.

Making good use of the twilight, she stood so the Gestapo guard had to look into the dropping sun. "What are you doing . . . a woman out at this hour of the evening?" he asked.

In flawless Italian she answered, "My husband is hopelessly drunk. I am afraid to go home. I have my sister near here. May I please pass?"

"Was sagen sie, Frau? I do not understand you . . ."

Mrs. Castelbaro repeated her statement in broken German. She waved her arms and began to cry.

The Gestapo police picked up her cheap suitcase and helped her over the border into Switzerland, lowering the long wooden barricade pole across the road behind her.

She reached Berne the next day. Vital messages were sent to Mr. Allen Welsh Dulles, head of American Intelligence in Western Europe.

Few American women spies worked in the same manner. One, known by the code name Lilian, danced at the Follies Bergere. Her lovely face and figure were attractive to war-weary officers of Hitler's army. Nightly she dated high-ranking personnel who carelessly spilled out information which proved highly interesting at Allied Headquarters.

In Shanghai there was another American woman at work in the tricky business of getting information from reliable sources. Rose de Saint Phalle was born in China and knew many of the country's dialects. She was dark-eyed, clever and sparkling, traits which helped her worm her way into the confidence and affection of Wang Shao-lai, the famous gunman and ranking top-dog of the Chinese underworld. He confided all his problems to her, from the personal ones centered around his seventeen wives and forty children, to the latest news of the Japanese politicians, military officers, collaborators and their secret service.

Whenever the OSS wanted information about Japanese influence in China, they went to Rose, who drew the truth from her influential Chinese friend. Obviously, the task was not easy nor was it always pleasant. There was constant danger of being found out, but Rose knew her position was helping the soldiers of the United States.

In London the OSS relied upon Louise Page Morris. She became a successful agent, not because she was beautiful, well dressed or brilliant, but because she was a good cook and warm, friendly human being.

During the "blitz" of London she remained in her small apartment and entertained the "right" people at small dinners prepared carefully on two old-fashioned gas burners. In some miraculous way Louise was nearly always able to procure the hard-to-find items of food—eggs, butter, sugar. As the buzz-bombs fell on London, the world's largest city, her guests were warm, well fed and became talkative. After each dinner party, Louise reported back to OSS.

Then there was a famous woman writer who traveled to Spain during the war. Her name is also a secret. The lady's assignment was to find out who, among the Spanish diplomats stationed in consular officers all over the world, were in the employ and pay of the Nazi government. The Germans were suspicious of her and almost certain of her activities, but there was very little they could do since Spain was a neutral country.

In addition to being famous as an authoress, this counter-spy was also beautiful. She succeeded in capturing the attention of one of General Franco's right-hand men. She kept him dangling with promises of marriage and an exciting life in the United States. Finally, one warm spring day, she sneaked aboard a ship and later arrived in New York with a list of twenty Spanish agents working for the Nazis in England and the Americas. Her temperamental lover committed suicide, but he never knew he had supplied the facts she wanted.

Among the professional spy catchers, perhaps the best of all American women agents was Mrs. Dorothy Huston. Wife of a former League of Nations official, she was a gifted actress and possessed, through her marriage, an understanding of international politics and a strong love of peace.

When the war began, Mrs. Huston's slim figure and smooth face made her appear younger than her forty-five years. People were surprised to learn she had three grandchildren. She spoke several languages, was gentle, resourceful and possessed one of the greatest talents of a spy . . . patience.

Her assignment started in London late in the year 1944.

A British Intelligence agent stationed at the Croyden airport saw a gentleman slip a letter to a male passenger as he boarded a plane bound for New York. The letter could have been harmless, but the fact that it by-passed censorship made it suspicious—perhaps dangerous.

Investigators, notified in New York, met the plane at La Guardia airport. They followed the man to an old brownstone house in the East Sixties in Manhattan.

Dorothy Huston was called to the OSS office by Frank Bielaski, chief of Counter Intelligence section.

After briefing her, Mr. Bielaski said, "Perhaps the man is a nobody. Perhaps he is not. We cannot afford to leave any stone unturned. Find out who he is and what he is doing."

Within two days the actress knew the London passenger was living with two foreigners in a small apartment on the third floor of the old brownstone house. She also learned that there was a vacant apartment next to theirs and a private school on the second floor.

Mrs. Huston told the headmistress of the school she had lost her husband in battle and landed a job as a teacher of French. This gave her every reason to move into the vacant apartment on the floor above.

Days passed and Mrs. Huston played the waiting game. When her neighbors passed her in the hall, she looked straight ahead without so much as saying hello.

At the end of the tenth day, one of her neighbors stopped her.

"Madame," he said, "we are neighbors. Perhaps you are lonely. We should get to know each other better. Will you drop in this afternoon for a cup of tea?"

Mrs. Huston said she was busy, but during the next days, she smiled and dropped courteous greetings when she met her suspects.

Three days later she was again invited by one of the men. This time she agreed to have tea with him alone.

Within two weeks, Mrs. Dorothy Huston was back in the office of the OSS.

"Mr. Belaski, my neighbors are Polish refugees actively engaged in espionage against the United States and the Allies. They have several agents working for them here, obtaining military information about troop shipments and new weapons. They are particularly interested in the Norden bomb sight. All their information goes into Germany by way of Argentina."

The entire spy ring was arrested during the next few weeks.

Nor was this the last of Mrs. Huston's assignments.

Vice-Admiral Eugenio Minsini of the Italian Navy had been captured, spirited out of Italy, and installed in a fashionable New York home. He was, however, watched by a crew of OSS agents posing as cooks, maids and valets. American Intelligence hoped the Admiral would be so pleased by this grand treatment that he would give them information about joint plans of the German and Italian military staffs. But the admiral refused, "I am a prisoner of war," he said, "not a traitor. I have nothing to say. Leave me alone." Nor did the eavesdropping by the household staff provide any useful facts.

The Intelligence Office called Mrs. Huston and explained their problem.

Mrs. Huston was introduced by an aristocratic Italian to Admiral and Signora Minsini. She used the name, Eileen Donnelly. The choice was no accident. The admiral's mother-in-law was Irish.

Eileen turned on the charm and a heavy Irish brogue. "Let me show you the sights of New York through the eyes of an Irish woman," she suggested to the admiral's wife. "We will go to mass at St. Patrick's Cathedral, one of the most beautiful churches in the world. And in March you must see our parade! You've never seen so much 'wearing of the green.' "

Signora Minsini was delighted to have a friend. She enjoyed the sight-seeing, the pleasant little restaurants and the busy life of New York. The women saw each other every day.

The opening came when Eileen learned the admiral hated the English. She said she agreed entirely. "The British," she replied, "are beasts, utterly selfish beasts. Why don't they give Ireland its independence instead of constantly crushing her under their heel?"

This was the beginning of anti-British raving that was melody to the admiral's ears. He liked her straightforwardness, her strong beliefs. His reserve faded. He began to talk, to talk about Italy, his past, his plans for the future. He mentioned names of those whom he trusted and those he mistrusted. He told of German strengths and outlined their weaknesses in Italy.

Mrs. Dorothy Huston, alias Eileen Donnelly, returned to Intelligence headquarters with all the information they wanted from their Italian visitor.

Near the end of the war Mrs. Huston asked to be released from service. Two years later she died of cancer.

When the announcement of her death was made, Soviet Intelligence did not believe it. "That statement does not fool us," they said. "Huston is merely working under another name."

At the beginning of the war when the United States Army was recruiting the "Thirty-day Wonders" from colleges and universities and putting them into officers' uniforms, women were also being contacted for spy work. Languages and knowledge of the world were needed, and a great number of socialites and debutantes were enlisted in the cloak-and-perfume ranks. The theory was that they had been abroad, had foreign contacts, and knew their way around.

On the whole, it did not work that way. Many of these women were spoiled children who could not do without luxuries. It was far more interesting to find an exciting European husband than to parachute into enemy territories. The men agents complained bitterly about these "society spies," and often felt they were more bother than they were worth. Sometimes, the men added, these women were hazards and risks to security.

The women more suited, emotionally and intellectually for the tasks of counter-espionage, came from sociology and political science departments of colleges, from newspaper offices and the Women's Army Corps and the Navy Waves.

Thirty-seven American women spies who worked in this shadowy world were daughters of missionaries.

Those women who possessed the moral timber and the brains to help the Allied efforts were rewarded at the end of the war by a statement made by Colonel Otto Doering, executive officer of the OSS: "In the face of extreme danger, the OSS women showed courage and ability on a par with any man's."

There was, for example, a woman agent operating inside Holland. She was betrayed and captured by fourteen Nazis, who beat her into a bleeding bundle.

Months later, when the Allies landed in the Netherlands, they went out in search for their missing agent. In a remote village they found Miss X, crippled for life, and mentally deranged.

It took years of loving care to restore life and hope to this Dutch citizens who worked for the United States Intelligence Service.

A happier story is that of a woman agent who parachuted into France in 1944 with the assignment to travel through Europe for five months, visiting various underground units.

After her jolting bounce on the solid ground of Europe, she tore off the bulky overalls, raced back to pick up a solidly made old straw suitcase, and wobbled down the road in the guise of an idiot peasant girl.

In her pocket she carried a bone with a liberal amount of meat on it. As she neared a village, she spotted a mongrel dog with a hungry look. She gave him the bone and a few friendly pats on his long, lean head. Together they continued down the narrow road. Her new companion was the final touch to her disguise.

On the outskirts of the town she was stopped by a Gestapo guard.

"Mademoiselle, what do you have with you?" he asked.

She held the bag behind her, giggled, and made half turns with her body like a ten-year-old being coy. "What do you think, Herr Officer, a machine gun? ? ? or perhaps a lover?"

The Nazi laughed and let her pass.

The American woman spy had short-wave radios, several cameras and guns in her beaten-up old straw suitcase.

Both General "Wild Bill" Donovan, the boss of the OSS, and his European spy chief, Colonel Russell Frogan, credit women with a lack of ego that makes them invaluable in the spy field.

"It never occurs to a woman," says Colonel Frogan, "to tell a man she is a big shot in the communications center or that she is a secret agent. Her desire is to interest a man for herself alone, not for the job.

"But the old saying holds true: if a woman falls in love with the man upon whom she is spying, she can no longer be trusted. Women realize this themselves. A good example is the OSS woman who was assigned to 'get next' to a German spy in London.

" 'Make him fall in love with you,' she was ordered, 'so he will reveal his contacts.'

"One day the girl reported to headquarters. 'I am worthless to you,' she said. 'I have not betrayed a thing, but I have fallen in love with the German officer. Send me home as fast as possible.' "

Since the war, United States Intelligence has changed some of its employment policies. They prefer happily married women. Any girl who has just passed through an unhappy love affair, may fall in love on the rebound. She can be putty in the hands of an enemy soldier if he is smart enough to flatter her. Unmarried women must have the professional attitude rather than the desire for marriage.

It is safe to estimate that hundreds of American girls are employed in intelligence work and one out of every ten agents is a woman.

The Soviets have long believed in women spies. Their percentage is, therefore, much higher.

But the romance has gone out of espionage for women. It is a cold, dirty, scientific job. There may be women secretaries or interpreters acting as agents at the UN or NATO meetings, women listening in the aircraft factories, women who carefully piece together bits of blueprints, but the days of the Old Vienna Congress, where whispers were exchanged behind the fan and notes were passed in the conservatories, are gone forever.

CHAPTER ELEVEN

The Microdot

Jimmy Bozart, a fourteen-year-old newsboy, clattered down the stairs of a Brooklyn apartment house, where he had been collecting from some of his customers, jingling a handful of change. He slipped and grabbed for the handrail. The nickels, dimes and quarters fell to the landing below.

Jimmy recovered the coins, his mind already on something else, until he picked up one of the five-cent pieces. It had split apart in the fall. The youngster noted that a tiny object had been wedged between the halves.

Here was real cloak-and-dagger spy stuff. When Jimmy showed his discovery to his father he was pleased that the older man was just as impressed as he was.

"This," Bozart senior ruled, "had better go to the police."

Jimmy agreed, giving the nickel to Patrolman Frank R. Milley, the father of one of his classmates.

Four years later, on August 7, 1957, a seedy, undistinguished man with faded blue eyes and wispy hair was indicted in the United States District Court in Brooklyn as one of the most important Soviet spies ever captured in the United States.

The two incidents—Jimmy Bozart's discovery of the split nickel and the arrest of Rudolf Ivanovich Abel, colonel of the overseas intelligence arm of the Soviet Union—are connected.

How close the connection is, we don't know. It may be years, if ever, before that information can be safely released. We do know that Patrolman Milley turned the nickel over to the F.B.I. We know that F.B.I. technicians found the object inside the coin was a microfilm of a card bearing six numbers. And we know that Jimmy Bozart, then preparing to enter college, was alerted to testify, if necessary, at Colonel Abel's trial.

The F.B.I. refused to discuss the precise importance of the nickel but said that, while it did not lead them directly to the Russian spy, it did help them complete the jigsaw puzzle of the Abel-directed espionage network.

The investigation that led to his arrest, conviction and a sentence of thirty years' imprisonment was probably typical of spy-catching. It included tracking down hundreds of tips, most of them false, observation, patient questioning of suspects, and piecing together thousands of seemingly unrelated items.

Colonel Abel's arrest by agents of the F.B.I. and the United States Immigration and Naturalization Service in July, 1957, caused little excitement. He was charged with illegal entry into the United States and placed in an alien detention camp in McAllen, Texas, to await deportation. The stranger-than-fiction story didn't come out until more than two weeks later, with his indictment.

Abel had been living as "Martin Collins" in Manhattan's little Latham Hotel off Fifth Avenue. He maintained a photographic and artist's studio on the top floor of a building at 252 Fulton Street, Brooklyn. The colonel had done what no writer of spy fiction would permit a character to do— that is, had operated directly across the street from the United States Courthouse.

While agents questioned Abel in Texas, others searched his "studio," turning up a treasure trove of evidence that convinced them their prisoner was no mere violator of immigration laws.

Residents in Fulton Street had known him as Emil R. Goldfus, a friendly man whose profession was photography and whose hobby was painting. He had a genuine talent and, one artist said, "would have been a very good painter within another five years."

He had entered this country in 1948 from Montreal under a false European passport that bore the name of Andrew Kayotis. It was only one of several aliases. Customarily, he carried birth certificates of Martin Collins, born on July 2, 1897, in New York City, and also of Emil R. Goldfus, an actual Manhattan infant who had been born August 2, 1902, and died two months later.

Well supplied with cash, he lived modestly, blending into the background of shabby hotels and his cluttered studio. He made friends with people, paid his rent on time, dropped into the Music Box for an occasional hamburger, and pleased nearby storekeepers by addressing them as "mister."

F.B.I. agents were not surprised to discover in his studio the tools of his supposed profession—cameras, lights and other photographic equipment. They did note with interest his powerful short-wave radio receiver, and other gear that was difficult to associate with an innocent photographer.

Altogether, they found 126 items in the Fulton Street studio, ranging from a blowtorch to glass cutters, batteries, hollowed-out nails, pencils, coins, cuff links and earrings; documents, powerful lenses and movie film. He was equipped to record messages in "microdots," a technique that enabled him to condense documents to the size of a pinhead. The agents refused to discuss their haul in detail.

Squads of G-men fanned out, following every lead, so far as possible, to its source. One item, for example, was a thank-you note from a Fulton Street acquaintance. Curious to learn how Abel had earned this person's gratitude, agents heard an explanation that satisfied them but did not help their case. The person in question had married recently and "Emil Goldfus" had sent a wedding gift. The couple was shocked to learn their well-wisher was Colonel Abel, of Russian Intelligence.

Other messages were suspicious. One handwritten note was obviously important:

"I bought a ticket for the next ship—*Queen Elizab.* for next Thursday, 1-31," it read. "Could not come because three men are tailing me."

Another: "In Mex — signal T pole opposite No. 191 Chihuahua st. using sides of pole toward roadway Sat. or Sun., Tues., Thurs. Met on Wed. Thur. Fri. 3 p.m. movie Balmora."

Still another: "Aneida Oberon 3 p.m. display left of entrance. Is this an interesting picture. Yes. Do you wish to see Mr. Brandt? Smokes pipe and has red book in left hand."

Abel's position in the Soviet espionage system was that of a Russian spy chief working in the United States in a way not yet fully exposed. He served as an executive, directing the work of others. He received his instructions from Moscow by short-wave radio. He then passed them along to members of his network, sending results to Soviet headquarters through an elaborate system of codes.

Some of the "drops" used by his co-workers for the transfer of information were revealed in notes found in his hotel room. They ranged as far off as Mexico. Some were of obvious interest to spies: Quincy, Massachusetts, is the site of an important shipyard and naval air station; New Hyde Park, Long Island, is near a plant producing electronic instruments for missile production. Agents were mystified, though, by Abel's assignment of a spy to Salida, Colorado, a small resort town in the heart of the Rocky Mountains.

Messages, both written and photographs, were passed in numerous containers such as the hollowed-out nails, coins and jewelry. In some cases, microscopic documents were carried to Russia by agents. Others may have been sent directly to the U.S.S.R.

It is doubtful whether any of the basic techniques used by Abel's branch office were unknown to the F.B.I. But they realized he was a dangerous man.

At the time of his arrest Abel was an espionage agent of some thirty years' experience. He probably was the most frightening foreign agent ever caught by United States counter-espionage, and there is no reason to believe Moscow does not have many more like him. He operated so smoothly that the amount of harm he did may never be established.

An expert photographer and cryptographer, he was also a trained electronics engineer, an accomplished sketcher and artist, and well trained in nuclear science.

In addition to his native language he speaks fluent English, French, German, and Italian.

The Russian Government and its Embassy in Washington ignored Abel's arrest and the colonel, as a professional, accepted his fate as that to be expected by a trapped spy.

Abel, when asked whether he wanted an attorney, requested a United States marshal to "contact Abt." The only lawyer of that name in the Manhattan directory is John J. Abt, counsel for United States Communists. In this case, however, Abt decided he was "too busy" to accept a new client.

Displaying his familiarity with American legal procedure, Abel appealed for a lawyer through the Brooklyn Bar Association. The organization went out of its way to find him a good one. They asked James B. Donovan, who served as wartime counsel for the Office of Strategic Services and who participated in the prosecution of Nazi leaders at Nuremburg.

The jury of nine men and three women was influenced by the story of an unexpected witness, M. Sgt. Roy A. Rhodes. He confessed he had betrayed secrets to Russia while working as a mechanic in the American Embassy in Moscow, for which he had recently been sentenced to five years.

Returned to the United States in 1953, Rhodes had agreed to continue his activities for Russia in this country under Abel's orders.

Abel, stony-faced and silent, heard his sentence on November 15, 1957. Judge Mortimer W. Byers fixed his penalty at thirty years' imprisonment, although he could have imposed a death sentence under the Espionage and Sabotage Act.

Just one day earlier, Russia broke the silence it had maintained since Abel's arrest. A Moscow literary newspaper that mentioned the case didn't discuss the evidence against Colonel Abel nor did it admit the existence of such a man.

It reported only that the F.B.I. had arrested an "artist-photographer named Goldfus" and then produced a piece of "low-brow crime fiction" to convict him. The purpose, Moscow explained, was to get the minds of the American people off "the dirty side" of the F.B.I.

And all this might never have happened if a sharp-eyed fourteen-year-old boy had not made his report of a strange finding.

CHAPTER TWELVE

The Man Who Sank the *Royal Oak*

One of the best-known German war heroes of the last world war was Captain Guenther Prien, who torpedoed the British battleship *Royal Oak* in October, 1939. The pride of the British Navy lay at anchor within the port of Scapa Flow which was thought to be completely protected by anti-submarine nets and cables. But the *Royal Oak* was sunk by the German submarine B-06, in the English harbor, taking eight hundred thirty-three sailors and officers to their deaths.

When the victorious Nazi submarine returned to its home base, a great celebration was given for Captain Prien and his crew. They were decorated, entertained and each was mentioned by name in the German papers.

In the midst of the home-coming, one man slipped away from the dock where the B-06 was moored. He wore no uniform. He wanted no part in the gaiety. He was the brilliant spy who made the successful attack on Scapa Flow possible.

His real name was Alfred Wehring. In the history of espionage few men can match his record. This is his remarkable story.

Sixteen years before the tragedy of Scapa Flow, Alfred Wehring, retired captain of the Imperial German Navy, left Germany. It was 1923, year of the Munich Beer Hall *Putsch,* year of the Nazi Free Corps. At that time Admiral Canaris, chief of the Nazi Secret Service, was living as an obscure officer. In reality he was engrossed in the task of reorganizing marine and military espionage for the "democratic" republic.

In 1923 Canaris sent out Germany's first naval spy since the Versailles Treaty had been signed. In those days nobody suspected what revolutions would be seen in Germany, or how the Ruhr Valley, then under occupation by the French, would change hands. Nor did they suspect World War II would come.

Alfred Wehring was one of the youngest captains in Germany. He had proved himself an able officer and was retained on the pay roll, in spite of the little work for him after 1919. Canaris had a high opinion of Alfred's abilities. In 1923, Canaris chose Wehring for an important new appointment. Wehring was to become a salesman for a German watch firm. He would visit many countries of Europe, and he was to watch out for new naval constructions.

After three years, Wehring was sent to Switzerland, where he became an apprentice to a Swiss watchmaking concern. In 1927 he emigrated to Britain. Nobody knew that he was a captain, or that he was German. He used the Swiss name of Albert Ortel.

He settled in Kirkwall on the Orkney Islands, close to the Scapa Flow base. The quiet district of Kirkwall needed a good watchmaker. Ortel worked in several small jewelry shops. His work was skillful, his charges small, and soon he became well known. Ortel lived modestly. He dreamed of opening his own little watch and gift shop in the heart of Kirkwall. There the sailors would purchase presents and souvenirs.

Eventually the dream was realized. Ortel became the owner of a shop selling gifts and Swiss watches.

The people liked their new neighbor. He was honest and pleasant. He was invited to their homes, on sailing and fishing jaunts, and to card games. In 1932 he became a British citizen.

Wehring had a great love for the sea. He was happy in this coastal town and never wanted to leave, even to make a trip back to Switzerland where his friends and family lived. Therefore, relatives and friends, all speaking with Swiss accents, came to see him during the summer months. Several decided that they, too, wanted to stay in England. Ortel assisted them in every way possible and found jobs in the district for them. The watchmaker received an abundance of mail from his relatives in Switzerland. He wrote at least once a month to his old father.

Actually, the "old father" was Admiral Canaris, and the numerous "relatives" were officers of the Nazi Secret Service. But Ortel was never suspected.

The life of Kirkwall was peaceful. Then the war broke out. Albert Ortel was the first to hang the English flag over his door, and he bought war certificates more frequently than the other citizens. "I'm far from neutral," he said to the neighbors. "I'm British now, not Swiss." He regretted that his age barred him from serving in the army. But he followed the war step-by-step, battle-by-battle. His radio was constantly tuned to war news.

Ortel was a great detective. It will never be known how he pieced together the information concerning the defenses of Scapa Flow.

But the facts are positive. A month after the outbreak of the war, Ortel learned the submarine traps and nets on the eastern approaches of Scapa Flow were not in place. They had been inspected and found to be unsound. Weakened by erosion the defenses had been removed.

Replacements of the underwater wall were ordered. They were on their way, but the confusion of the war, plus ordinary red tape, held up the shipment. Ortel knew the nets and traps were not in place. The replacements would take a few days, and Scapa Flow was defenseless during that time.

On the October day when the watchmaker discovered this important fact, he closed shop a little earlier than usual. "It's raining, and we'll have no more customers," he explained to his assistant. He closed the iron shutters and went home.

Albert's home was cozy and thoroughly British. On the hearth a bright fire burned. Albert turned on the radio to get the war news. Then he went to his closet and produced a pair of earphones. The closet seemed to contain an old-fashioned radio set, with the awkward dials and knobs of bygone years. It was a short-wave transmitter. Ortel spun a knob, adjusted a dial, and spoke slowly into the mouthpiece.

The message was sent to the German naval attaché in neutral Holland. From The Hague the message was speedily forwarded to Canaris, who learned the essential fact that Scapa Flow was defenseless and wide open for a submarine attack.

The very same hour Canaris acted. Code instructions were sent out to Nazi submarines in the North Sea and the Channel. The German naval attaché in Holland was instructed to contact Ortel—Wehring—in Kirkwall.

Captain Guenther Prien of submarine B-06 was selected to do the job. He was ordered to bring his submarine to the surface close to the easternmost tip of Pomona Island. It was a dark night, with thick fog.

As the submarine came nearer and nearer to the coast, Prien gave orders for the motor of the submarine to be shut off. He lifted his glasses and scanned the vague outline of the coast. Through the fog, he caught sight of a light. Yes, it was the agreed signal—one long, two short, one long. It was the signal Canaris had fixed.

Captain Guenther Prien ordered the collapsible rubber boat to be lowered and manned by one sailor. A "friend" was to be rescued from England. It was not long before Prien shook hands with watchmaker Ortel-Wehring, who was brought on board the submarine. The submarine dived.

Ortel handed over his information. He had prepared naval maps of every yard of Scapa Flow. He pointed out where the defenseless parts lay. Prien took the map and gave his orders. The submarine cut through the water like a shark dodging the known obstacles of Scapa Flow.

Through the fog, the periscope showed the massive bodies of several light cruisers and destroyers. But Prien was looking for the big ship that lay farthest away. It was the great battleship *Royal Oak*.

The engines stopped. The periscope was fixed to give a perfect image of the *Royal Oak*. Prien gave the signal.

"Fertig, schiessen" was the command, and the first torpedo made its fatal flight towards the *Royal Oak*. They heard a fearful explosion. A second torpedo was launched. The periscope revealed the *Royal Oak* burning and sinking inside Britain's safest harbor.

The 29,150-ton ship sank swiftly. Only 396 of her crew of 1,200 were saved.

Captain Prien was proud of their night's work, but Wehring could not share his joy. He had given his service to Germany, but the men who were drowning had often been in his little shop in Kirkwall. They bought gifts for their mothers, children and sweethearts. And this was how he was repaying their friendship.

Perhaps he told Canaris how he felt, for he never did another job of espionage.

CHAPTER THIRTEEN

Tokyo Rose: Traitor in Pigtails

In a San Francisco courtroom, watching the trial of the 33-year-old Iva Toguri, it seemed, in a flash, that I understood her. That girl was a traitor for probably no other reason than it was all she could do under the circumstances. It was a job that did not pay much, but it fed her.

There was hardly any great scheme behind it. Someone in Japan had offered her the job and she took it. The war was on; she could not return to America; she needed money badly. If she did not take that job she would have been interned as an enemy alien in Japan.

It was all so confusing to her. What had she ever known of politics? Nothing! She was interested in drama, voice, speech. She had loved it at the University of California at Los Angeles. She was a native American, second generation Japanese.

In 1941 she had an invitation to go to Japan. Her sick aunt and uncle lived in Tokyo and she wanted to see Japan— war or no war. America was not in the war yet, though the

State Department warned all Americans not to travel to Japan.

They even refused to issue passports, so young Iva went without one.

Later, in Japan, she faced the bitter fact that she could not return to America. She had missed the last chance, for while she was searching for transportation home to her parents, who ran a grocery store in Chicago, bombs fell on Pearl Harbor—and America was in the war.

"I could not believe it," she said. "I was dazed for many days. Then I was arrested by the Japanese as an enemy alien, but later released."

Iva bought her freedom for a price. A high price: Treason. The former zoological research student of the University of California became known to every soldier in the Pacific as *Tokyo Rose*.

First she went on the air as Ann, then she changed her name to "Orphan Annie, your playmate." She opened her programs with the provoking words, "Good evening again to the . . . forgotten men, the American fighting men . . ." Fascist Japanese propaganda was mixed with American jazz and popular songs.

Her wages at the beginning were very small, not more than one hundred yen, less than ten dollars a month . . . "Which," she says, "was not enough to live on." Later it was raised to one hundred and forty-seven yen.

Iva claims she was forced into this work. She also told a love story. The man who forced her to this kind of treacherous propaganda was very fond of her, and she did not dare reject him. It was the old story. Iva went the easiest way, as many a woman agent has done in many a war.

Early in the Pacific war Tokyo Rose had a tremendous listening audience. It was new to the American soldiers. Their radio sets could not get American stations, so Tokyo was the next best. Both Tokyo Rose and the Japanese knew this.

The boys were craving to hear American dance music. Tokyo Rose gave it to them. In turn came her propaganda and subversive talks, well prepared by these grave-diggers of democracy.

Once when the Americans were working feverishly and secretly on an airfield in the Marshall Islands, Tokyo Rose came on the air, identified the islands, told the soldiers they would be bombed soon, and jokingly added: "Confidentially, boys, your strip is showing." She ended the announcement with a nasty, cynical laugh.

"Hi, boys . . . this is your old friend," she once broadcasted. "I've got some swell new recordings for you, just in from the States. You'd better enjoy them while you can, because tomorrow at 0600, you're hitting Saipan . . . and we're ready for you. So, while you're still alive, let's listen to . . ."

Other broadcasts followed in the same vein. During the zero hour of American landings in the Pacific, she said:

"You boneheads of the Pacific, if you expect to get home you'd better start now. Haven't you heard the fleet is about gone?"

"I wonder who your wives and girl friends are out with tonight, maybe some 4-F (medical category meaning unfit for service)."

"The Americans have lost all their ships at Leyte Gulf and don't know how they'll get home."

Iva was sure she would never be detected. There were seven American and Canadian women doing these broadcasts. She was only one of the seven voices. When, after VJ day, she was sitting in the dining room of the very fashionable Bund Hotel in Tokyo, the Japanese betrayed her. So did her own familiar voice.

Later, she sat in front of the three American soldiers who had arrested her. "I'm innocent," she said. "I have done . . . nothing." She behaved like the little schoolgirl and looked like one. One soldier said, "If she had been on television, she wouldn't have lasted a week."

She sat there in girlish pigtails, dressed like a teen-ager, wide-eyed, smiling, wondering. She could not believe that she had done anything wrong.

Clerk Lee, a former war correspondent, testified at the trial that when he had interviewed Tokyo Rose in September, 1945, and asked her if she didn't feel she was doing wrong in broadcasting enemy propaganda, she replied: "I had no particular feeling about it."

She probably spoke the truth when she also told the reporter: "I needed the extra hundred yen they paid me."

Her trial lasted for twelve weeks. The Government compiled two million words of testimony. It flew nineteen witnesses from Japan, including high-ranking Japanese officers. The evidence was overwhelming.

Yet Iva declared she was innocent and was forced into the job. If she had wanted to be a traitress she would have become a Japanese citizen. She had never tried to undermine the bravery of the American soldier, or told lies or given secret coded messages.

Besides, she pointed out, she had married a Portuguese in 1945, and was now a Portuguese citizen. As a foreigner she could not commit treason against the United States. It was a confused defense, trying always to protect the "little child" who was thrown into treason without knowing it.

Then the Government replayed the records of her broadcasts. It was a surprise. The defense never expected that move. The courtroom was taken back into the atmosphere of war.

After Rose said she was not guilty, she had never done harm with her words to anyone, the records spun out her ugly words: "Orphans of the Pacific . . . how will you get home? . . . now that all your ships are sunk?" and the cynical laughter again.

One record after another was played. They proved open treason, incitement to revolt, playing up to race-hatred and bigorty, saying that Negroes should not die for white men in the American forces—the old Fascist routine.

The jury deliberated for a long time. Tokyo Rose did not wear pigtails any longer. Her hair had a permanent wave, and she was dressed in a light-colored suit.

She looked questioningly at the jury when they entered the courtroom. Would they sentence her to death? No, it was impossible in her mind. Up to the last minute she was sure she would be freed. She had been forced into that job. Words over the radio did not kill anyone; it was like in a play.

The verdict came as a shock to her: Ten years and $10,000 fine.

"No, this is not possible," she cried. "I can't believe you would send me to jail."

But they did.

CHAPTER FOURTEEN

Guatemalan Incident

The world of Otto Lange had never extended beyond the frontiers of Europe and certainly not as far as Central America and the Republic of Guatemala. Yet this stocky, middle-aged German was responsible in 1954 for the downfall of the Guatemalan government — an almost bloodless revolution achieved by remote control.

Otto Lange was not his real name. His hidden identity is of no consequence. Of the known facts it seems he was born in Koenigsberg in East Prussia, which today is a Russian city. From the very start Lange was involved in the growth of Communism. He fell in step so easily that he was recognized as a reliable follower and called to Moscow for indoctrination and training.

After the war he worked under the Red flag in East Germany and was then sent to Poland to help the People's Republic rebuild the country's heavy industry. He possessed a wide technical knowledge and was a skilled organizer. Under his guidance, and with the help of forced labor, many factories reopened. Otto became a key figure wherever expansion took place. One of Lange's biggest jobs was the rebuilding of the machine-tool works at Stettin, the capital of Pomerania which once had a population of 150,000. Lange found there were less than 5,000 Germans living there but many Russians and Poles watched over by political commissars.

Nobody escaped the attention of the commissars, not even Lange, although he had many times been "cleared" by the Secret Service. Conforming to Party discipline, he never allowed himself to become involved in it, but he was respected for his loyalty and his devotion to work.

Lange had married an attractive Polish girl and was the father of two children. His home life was above question, after the Bolshevik model. His only extravagance was the leisure time he gave to outdoor sports. He loved hunting and fishing and, occasionally, he would take the family out for a day's boating in small motor launch he owned.

But on that lovely early season day in April, 1954, when Otto Lange sat on the bank of the Oder River, overlooking the harbor at Stettin, he was alone with a fishing rod, a picnic basket of food and a pair of field glasses. During the hours he remained there, Lange paid little attention to his fishing, but would raise his field glasses to watch the birds in the sky. Then he would watch the harbor where many freighters were being loaded for the return journey to Soviet Russia through the wide Baltic. Anyone watching Lange would have thought he was a lazy fisherman. No one would have guessed the field glasses contained a built-in camera which was taking a record of what was happening in the harbor.

Later that afternoon Lange returned to his large, comfortable office in Stettin. Not one fish lay in his basket, but he appeared to be extraordinarily cheerful. He dictated a report to his superiors in Warsaw, a number of letters to trade combines in Dresden and East Germany and another letter to a firm in Paris interested, apparently, in the products of the factory which Lange controlled.

This letter, written in French and padded with commercial jargon, was carefully composed. It quoted prices for various automobile parts, the stock available and a proposed date for delivery. Certain tool-making machines were offered for sale and the letter said that, once equipped with such machinery, the French company would be able to do its own manufacturing by paying a fee to Lange's department of the Polish Ministry of Machine Industry.

The letter ended with assurances that the new Poland would fulfill all contracts. It pointed out that the Government was anxious to encourage commercial relations between the East and the West. The prices quoted were considerably lower than could be obtained elsewhere and certainly underbid those of Britain and America.

But the deal never came off. Six months later the Communists in Poland learned that Otto Lange and his secretary were spies whom the Americans had placed in Stettin. The model business letter to a Paris firm had been a coded message directed to one of the secret offices of America's Central Intelligence Agency in Paris.

Having reached its Parisian address, the letter was taken to a *salon de photographie* where American microfilm technicians set to work on it. The job was relatively simple if you knew what to look for. The microfilm specialists studied every period in the letter. They scratched each one carefully as they came to it until they found a black dot which could be scratched off the page. It was really a tiny speck of microfilm which had been glued on to look like a period.

When the microfilm enlarger was used it produced a readable message, ready to be passed on to the proper intelligence department analyst. It was in code. The microfilm technician was completely in the dark as to its meaning. All he saw was a cryptogram which used one of the most beautiful psalms of David: "My God, my God—why hast thou forsaken me?"

The coded message was flown to Allen Welsh Dulles, director of America's Central Intelligence Agency in Washington. It was promptly decoded and then returned to Dulles' desk. The message described the new underground route by which armaments were to be shipped to Latin America. The port of origin was Stettin on the Baltic Sea. A Swedish freighter had been loaded with 15,000 crates and boxes which had recently arrived by rail from Czechoslovakia. They contained ammunition. The freighter had been chartered from a reputable firm in Stockholm, who knew nothing of this traffic. The business arrangements had been made through a shipping agent in London who had re-chartered the vessel. The cargo was supposed to consist of optical instruments destined for French West Africa. But Otto Lange had revealed the true facts and made it plain that the ship and its cargo was not intended for West Africa.

It was a valuable piece of information. American counter-intelligence found means of letting Lange know that his message had been received and properly understood. He had done his work well and was advised to escape from Stettin as quickly as he could. He was told to make his way with his family to West Berlin where he would be protected. Lange got away, together with his wife and family and his trusted secretary.

To those who were awaiting him in West Berlin, Lange gave a fuller account of his discovery concerning the freighter. He had guessed that it was bound for Guatemala, but he had to satisfy himself that his hunch was right. All he had to go on was certain information he had picked up in the Ministry of Commerce. Every official document showed the ship's destination as Africa. But Lange had two friends aboard the ship. They had taken a look at the cargo and found the crates packed with small arms and machine guns.

Two days before the Swedish vessel was due to reach Africa, a shortwave message in code was received by the Central Intelligence Agency. The news was that the *Alfhem* was changing course and heading for Honduras.

The ship and its dangerous cargo now became a matter of concern for the intelligence department of the U. S. Navy. Communist weapons were being smuggled into the Western Hemisphere. Emergency sessions were held in Washington. London was notified. The U. S. fleet stationed in the Caribbean was put on the alert and submarines received special orders. The *Alfhem* never landed. Two days out the captain of the vessel received new orders. He was to proceed to Puerto Barrios, the Caribbean port of Red Guatemala.

The United States had no legal power to halt the vessel and take the arms. Moreover, Washington was eager to learn the strength of the Communist conspiracy in Guatemala. If the United States was to back the opposition in Guatemala, it had to know what resources the existing government had on hand.

It was hard to let the shipment pass. On the other hand, the incident could be used as a lever by which the Communists could be ousted from the Republic of Guatemala once and for all. There was also some danger for Mr. Dulles' department. If the secret leaked out the public would be sure to accuse Dulles of sheltering Communists.

* * * * *

The Communists in the Guatemalan Ministry of Defense were present at the docks when the *Alfhem* was unloaded at Puerto Barrios. The harbor area had been sealed off and was under guard. The crates and boxes were loaded on military trains.

A few hours later Washington had its first report from Guatemala. The 15,000 boxes and crates contained 1,900 tons of small arms and ammunition. Armed in this way the Communists in Guatemala would have been able to overrun the neighboring republics of Honduras and El Salvador. They could then march through Nicaragua and Costa Rica and on to the Panama Canal.

It was May 17, 1954.

When the United States presented these significant facts to the governments of Nicaragua, Costa Rica, El Salvador and Honduras, they were so alarmed that they asked America to intervene. But this was not what America desired, not what Dulles had planned.

Order followed order. A huge fleet of America's latest super Globemasters ferried twenty-five tons of rifles, machine-guns, pistols and hand grenades to Honduras and Nicaragua. Destruction of Communism in Central America was the goal of the master plan.

It was, too, the moment for Colonel Carlos Castillo Armas, a former officer of the Guatemalan Army, exiled in Honduras, to go into action. Colonel Armas was now able to rally every anti-Communist refugee in Central America to his cause. He armed those who were willing to fight the Communists in Guatemala and began the armed invasion of the country.

The resignation of the Red puppet president was demanded. Colonel Armas sent two outworn aircraft over Guatemala City.

Then came the biggest surprise of all. The Communist stronghold fell overnight. The war had not lasted twenty-four hours when the army went over to the side of Colonel Armas. The army accepted the support of the neighboring republics and the U.S.A., and made a clean sweep of the Communist elements in their midst. The Reds had delivered them the weapons with which they hoped to extend their Soviet domain, but quick action by democratic forces had curbed their ambitions. Credit is due to Otto Lange. Now he is working in a far-away country inside the Soviet Zone, visiting port after port to build up harbor espionage system for the Allies.

The Russians did not take their defeat calmly. Ilya Ehrenburg, the keenest of the Soviet propagandists said, "Even if the spy Allen Welsh Dulles should arrive in heaven through somebody's absentmindedness, he would begin to blow up the clouds and slaughter the angels."

The wisecrack got back to Allen Welsh Dulles. He laughed and replied dryly: "That may well be. But I hardly expect to discover any Red angels up there!"

CHAPTER FIFTEEN

The Red Chrysanthemum

The early spring of 1955 found the world seeing red. The Chinese had occupied the Tachen Islands. Dag Hammerskjold had flown from the United Nations building in New York straight to Red China's Chou En-Lai to plead for a cease fire in the Straits of Formosa.

During this time of crisis Eva Wu wrote her own spy history. Though it was a genuine drama it sounds like something straight out of a Grade B Hollywood movie.

Eva Wu lived in Hong Kong. This British Crown colony and the neighboring Chinese city of Kowloon are the spy centers of the Far East, just as Berlin, Stockholm or Vienna are in Europe. In Hong Kong information is exchanged; plots are evolved; people are kidnapped and murdered almost every day in the name of international intrigue. The agents of Chiang Kai-Shek and Mao Tse-Tung are constantly engaged in silent struggles there. In the meantime the world watches the headlines and wonders if a spark from Asia will ignite yet another and, perhaps, the final, world war.

Eva Wu, an exotic Oriental dancer, has a remarkable

tale to tell. For months, in spite of close supervision by Communist counter-spies, she succeeded in sending reports out of Red China.

But to begin her story where it started, Eva, whose figure and charm personified Oriental beauty at its most exciting, had had an engagement in one of the night clubs in Hong Kong. Night after night she danced famed old temple dances for the entertainment of an international crowd of men and women. Because of her great success she was enjoying a life of ease. Then back in May, 1954, as she hurried out of the club at the end of a performance, a voice spoke to her out of the darkness: "Would you like to serve your country?"

The dancer was frightened, but only for a moment. Somehow this man's voice sounded kind. As her eyes became adjusted to the darkness, she saw that he wore European clothing and limped badly.

"Ah, a wounded veteran," she thought, and felt sympathy for him. She followed and sat down beside him on a dark bench near the waterfront.

He spoke like an educated Cantonese, and Eva ceased to wonder why she trusted this stranger. These were difficult times. She, too, was one of the many hundred thousands of of refugees who had lost her homeland. Her father had been a doctor in Canton and the head of a family of fifteen children, but he had been able to provide a university education for his promising daughter, Eva. When the Communists conquered the country, slice by slice, her father had given Eva a few ounces of gold. She made her way through the country to Hong Kong. In her mind there had always been the nagging question: "What can I do to help? What can I do to rid the country of the Communists?" Perhaps this stranger in the dark could tell her what to do. It was even possible that he carried a message from her brothers or some news of her family.

Somehow Eva felt new hope when her companion began to tell her about herself. He knew where she had lived, about her family in Canton, and where her room was now. He spoke easily and calmly. At last she interrupted him. "But you said I could be of help. What can I do?"

"From time to time you go into the Chinese city to shop," he said. "Here is a letter I would like you to deliver to a certain place outside the British Crown Colony. I cannot take it myself. The place is swarming with spies, and I am too well known."

"That doesn't sound very difficult," Eva replied.

The lame stranger explained the dangers, but the dancer agreed. It was arranged between them that he would bring letters to her and she would smuggle them into the Chinese city. On every trip she would inform him if everything had worked out all right. If things went well on her visit, she would wear a white flower in her hair while she danced at the club. If it were necessary to warn him there had been a slip-up, she would wear a red flower instead.

The following day Eva carried out her first mission. She hid the letter in her mass of sleek hair, which she piled in loops on her head in the style of figures in old Japanese prints. Her shopping expedition was uneventful, and it was easy to give the letter to the shopkeeper.

From then on she continued to take the letters from the International Settlement to the Chinese section. Through their meetings, Eva learned that the lame man was an officer in the Nationalist Secret Service. She was introduced to the new science of communication. Later, her messages were delivered on small microfilms. Eva never read them, and was never aware of what information she carried. Once she took parts of a short-wave radio set to a silk store in the Chinese city.

Eva Wu's innocent shopping trips in the Chinese city for feminine fineries, silks and brocades, perfumes and sequins, successfully hid orders to Chiang Kai-Shek's underground men, microfilmed reports of secret troop movements and of the arrival of Soviet arms, and planned commando raids against the Nationalist-held islands. Glamorous Eva Wu had become an important link in China's war of spies and counter-spies. She informed Formosan headquarters a few hours after a Polish ship had left the China coast or about the departure of new opium transports for ports in Asia. Eva became the most important spy carrier in that area for Chiang Kai-Shek's underground. Anyone watching her finger a roll of blue brocade or select a new costume would hardly have suspected that this fragile feminine beauty was a sharp knife in the vital network of Communist activities.

For six months everything went well. Eva was never disturbed or fearful of discovery. What she was doing seemed to be simple. Her "spy boss," the lame officer, remained near her, kind and gentle, and cautioned her always to be careful. She developed a great admiration for him, and was grateful when he brought her news that two of her brothers were safe with the Nationalist troops on Formosa. She was glad that she, too, could help in some small way.

In the unlit underground of espionage, she was an important agent. In the bright lights of the nightclub, ivory-skinned

Eva rapidly climbed to heights as the most famous dancer in all Hong Kong. Her audience was fascinated by her Oriental dances. Her success lay in her skillful blending of authentic ritual with her own modern interpretations. She captivated her audiences in an almost hypnotic way.

A great favorite of the public was a dance of exorcism, a temple dance to keep away the evil spirits. In one hand she carried a jade-handled dagger and in the other a twinkling brass bowl of water. With slow gestures she clearly gave the impression that she was purifying the audience, herself and all the land of Confucius. There were times when, at the end of her dance, the audience had become so engrossed in the dance that seconds would pass before they could applaud.

And so Eva's life flowed peacefully. She lived in rich comfort, stayed away from friends, and was seen only with her "cousin," the lame man. She studied the dance, and explored new music for her uses. Her spy work took little of her time, for she was asked to deliver messages seldom more than twice a month.

But one day in February, 1955, during Eva's trip into the old Chinese city, she was stopped by two well-dressed men who said they were agents of the police. They insisted that she would have to be searched. Eva gave a point-blank refusal. The men pushed her into a waiting car, and she was driven to the police station. There she was undressed by a Red police matron and searched from head to foot. But they found nothing.

"You have no right to do this," she said, haughtily. "I am a dancer. All I am interested in is the dance and art— and I do not meddle with politics. You have no right to act as you have done. I demand that you release me at once."

The Communist agents grinned, but they were not amused. "Dance, art—*and* that swine Chiang Kai-Shek! Two of your brothers work for him, and you, too, are probably a spy. Dancer, we have watched you for many weeks."

They let her go. The undiscovered message she had been carrying had been put down on a tiny point, the tiny, tiny strip of microfilm on a single needle and silk thread that lay in her handbag. Once again, she had been able to deliver her vital report—orders to help the Nationalist commando raiders at their next landing. It had been a close call.

It was a proud Eva who stepped upon the stage that night and carefully wound the temple robes in folds about her feet. She had fooled the enemy. She began her most famous dance with her left hand on the dagger held in her gold sash and her right hand tenderly lifting the bright engraved brass bowl. Slowly the stage lights brightened, shooting a thousand tiny sparks off her jeweled robe. Her face, masked in white paint, eyes lined until they appeared twice their actual size, was immobile as she began her slow movements.

Eva half turned her body to extend the bowl for purification to the audience. At that moment she saw the two agents who had arrested her only a few hours before. Wildly she knew that she was in deadly peril. She became gripped by panic. She feared she might drop the bowl. At all costs she must be calm and not betray herself. Fighting to recover her poise, she turned slowly, in a half crouch, to face the other side of the room.

There at a table sat her friend, the lame man. She was trapped between friend and foe, and unable to signal her danger. With tiny steps she continued to dance, following the ever-quickening tempo of the wood-wind orchestra and the temple drum beat. As the music became ever faster in response to her movements, Eva tried to think of a way out. She knew her life was in danger, but to try to escape would invite a bullet in her back. Foolishly she had ignored the events of the afternoon and her arrest. She was wearing a white chrysanthemum instead of a red one.

The orchestra had stopped playing but Eva, clinging to precious moments, continued to dance, and in whirling steps stopped in the center of the stage. The temple drummer followed her steps with his beat. The audience was held by her power and sat spellbound by this new addition to her dance.

Kneeling slowly, Eva placed the bowl on the floor before her. With head upturned as if praying, she tore the dagger from her sash and cut a gash along the length of her left forearm. Taking the white flower from her hair, she ran the blossom along the wound as if she were feeding its white purity into her life's blood. It turned crimson—for danger.

Then, for the first time, she smiled. The audience thought it was merely the end of her act. She stretched her bleeding left arm straight before her and held high over her head in her right hand the blood-red chrysanthemum.

The audience, sitting in a death-like silence, awoke from its spell and broke into thunderous applause. A few, as they clapped, whispered among themselves about Eva's latest "trick."

The crowd was still applauding when Eva's "spy boss" entered her dressing room. His hands shook as he wrapped a cloak around her. "Very clever," he said. "Hurry, we must get away. Here, out the back alley."

In the light of one street lamp, Eva saw the two figures of

the Red Chinese police. They safely made their way to her "cousin's" parked car and drove to the nearest hospital.

People in Hong Kong still talk about Eva Wu and remember her last show. They say that of all her great dances, the night she drained her blood was the most dramatic. They wonder why she is never seen in the city's clubs any more. Some say she is dancing in San Francisco. Some even say she was killed—but a number of people report having seen Eva on Formosa, holding hands with a lame man.

CHAPTER SIXTEEN

The Lady with the Dolls

The scene opens in the autumn of 1943, during World War II, some thirteen hours' train journey from New York, in Springfield, Ohio, there lived a respected old family, the Wallaces. Miss Mary Wallace had never thought about spies a great deal. She was more interested in the arts than in politics. One morning she received an airmail letter from Argentina. The address, however, was not to Mary Wallace, but to:

Senor Inez Lopez de Molinali,
2563 O'Higgins Street,
Buenos Aires, Argentina

How on earth did this letter, addressed to some unknown person in Argentina, get into Mary Wallace's post box? She puzzled over it a minute. Turning the letter over she saw the back flap gave the return address as:

Mary Wallace,
1808 E. High Street,
Springfield, Ohio

The envelope was typewritten and carried, besides the

Argentine postmark, that of "Grand Central Station," New York, dated a month earlier. Here was certainly a mystery, Miss Wallace had never sent the letter, nor had she any friend named de Molinali in Argentina. In fact, she knew nobody in Latin America.

She opened the envelope and read the letter. It was written in her name, but she could not make head or tail of the contents. The signature read "Mary Wallace," and the stationery resembled hers, but was plainly not. How had this letter come to her? Again she examined the envelope and noticed the Argentine postal message: "Moved. Left no forwarding address. Return to sender."

Evidently, someone had written to Senora de Molinali in Argentina and had used the name of Mary Wallace. The Latin lady had not been at the given address, and the letter had been returned to the real Mary Wallace. She was puzzled and annoyed. Who had dared to use her name and forge her signature? The letter was full of misspellings and was written in poor English. She read the letter with growing anger. This was the strange text:

Dear Friend:

you probably wonder what has become of me as I havent written to you for so long. We have had a pretty bad month or so. My little nephew the one I adore so has a tumor on the brain and isnt expected to live, so we're all crushed that we dont know what we are doing. They are giving him exray on the head and they hope to check it but give us absolutely no hope in a complete cure and maybe not even any relief. I am completely crushed.

You asked me to tell you about my collection a a month ago. I had to give a talk to an Art Club so I talked about my dolls and figurines. The only new dolls I have are three lovely Irish dolls. One of these three dolls is an old Irish fisherman with a net over his back another is an old woman with wood on her back and the third is a little boy.

Everyone seemed to enjoy my talk I can only think of our sick boy these days.

You wrote me that you had sent a letter to Mr. Shaw he distroyed your letter, you know he has been ill. His car was damaged but is being repaired now. I saw a few of his family about. They all say Mr. Shaw will be back to work soon.

I do hope my letter is not too sad. There is not much I can to write you these days.

I came in this short trip for Mother on business before I make out her income tax report that is also WHY I am learning to type. Everyone seems busy these days the streets are full of people.

Remember me to your family sorry I havent written to you for long.

Truly

Mary Wallace

PS Mother wanted to go to Louville but due to our worry the Louville plan put out our minds now.

Miss Wallace was puzzled. There were startling features in this letter. It was true her nephew had a serious brain ailment. It was also true she had lectured to a club in Springfield about her art collection. But she had no Irish dolls. She had certainly not been in New York when the letter to Argentina was posted. Finally, she never used a typewriter, but wrote all her letters by hand.

She decided that someone was playing a poor joke on her, making sport of her habit of collecting dolls. Mary Wallace turned the letter over to the postal authorities to find out who was behind the senseless trick.

The Springfield postmaster forwarded the letter to the F.B.I. In Washington it was carefully studied. They felt it was too strange to be innocent and too pointless to be a joke. Its contents had not disturbed the postal censor, who may have thought it merely illiterate and confused. On the surface the letter was harmless, but the false return address raised questions. One Washington agent had a definite theory. It might be all wrong, but it was worth an investigation.

Agent B's thought was that the "new dolls" were code words for warships operating in the Pacific. "Irish fisherman" could mean an aircraft carrier because the carrier was draped in safety nets. The old woman with wood on her back might stand for a warship with wooden superstructure, and the little boy doll, a new destroyer.

The Mr. Shaw who had "destroyed the letter" could be the USS Shaw which had almost been demolished in the Pearl Harbor attack. This destroyer had been repaired and given a new bow at Honolulu. It now made the run between the Hawaiian Islands and San Francisco.

As for the postscript, the agent made the wild guess that it referred to the USS Louisville, a cruiser which had been at sea a long time, and whose whereabouts was a closely guarded secret. The postscript seemed to say that requested information could not be given.

It was a fantastic analysis. The postal censors refused to believe it. But, once the case had been opened, all relevant material was laid on the F.B.I. desks in Washington.

Mary Wallace was questioned. She told Agent B about her doll collection. She had recently added to it during a trip to New York. She had bought several dolls at America's select doll shop on Madison Avenue near 62nd Street. She had chatted quite a while with the woman who ran the store.

"Did you speak about family matters to the store owner?" asked Agent B.

"Well, yes, I did," answered Mary Wallace. "Mrs. Dickinson was very nice. She gave me a doll at a bargain price. Her collection is very beautiful and genuine."

"Did you mention anything about your nephew's brain ailment?"

"Yes. You see Mrs. Dickinson spoke with deep feeling of her husband's last months of life. It brought to my mind the condition of our nephew, who is seriously ill."

But this was not enough evidence to arrest Mrs. Dickinson. Miss Wallace listed at least ten other people who knew about her doll collection and the illness of her nephew. The doll store was only one of many clues. Agent B was interested in checking them all. He sensed the letter was dangerous. It was strange that the letter writer was such a poor speller. Yet, in spite of the many errors, it seemed to have been written by an American.

The dolls interested him. Therefore, he began his search among Mary Wallace's acquaintances in the art clubs, hobby groups and doll shops.

In Springfield, he started at the art club where Mary Wallace had lectured. But he gathered nothing from his interviews. The people appeared to be unconscious of any world outside Springfield, Ohio. No one had any connections in Argentina.

It was going to be tough, Agent B thought, but he was a careful operator and had plenty of time. He felt this letter was not the only one. He ordered the postal censor to stop every letter which made any mention of dolls or doll trade. Ordinary business letters of this description were held up and forwarded to Agent B for study. He wanted to get a clear picture of the doll import and export business.

Agent B traveled to New York for a visit to the doll shop on Madison Avenue. It was a luxury store for wealthy doll fanciers and collectors of antique toys. Its blue letterheads read:

Velvalee Dickinson

Dolls - Antique - Foreign - Regional

The stock was rare and expensive. Antique dolls from the colonial period brought five hundred dollars apiece. The store resembled a cross between an art museum and a marionette show. There were porcelain beauties dating from the Paris of Victor Hugo, exquisite Marie Antoinette figurines, and stolid wooden dolls from the American frontier. There were carved idols made by natives of Dutch Guinea as playthings for their children. Round-faced, delicately tinted dolls from China sat on a shelf. The window held a mixture of dolls, some toy horses, clay animal figures and children's tiny furniture, beautifully arranged.

The owner, Velvalee Dickinson, was an attractive widow

less than five feet tall, with a bright smiling face. She did not look fifty years old.

F.B.I. agents came to her store but asked no direct questions. They posed as customers and kept their eyes open. They lingered and looked but bought nothing.

Next, an investigation of Velvalee Dickinson's background was started. The F.B.I. collected some facts from the West Coast. She was better known there, for until 1937, when her husband died, she had lived in California.

Born in Sacramento, she had studied at Stanford University. Her maiden name was Malvena Blucher, which might indicate kinship to the Prussian General Blucher who fought against Napoleon. She had no criminal record, but her name appeared on the membership list of the American-Japanese Society which she belonged to as late as 1937. Her late husband had his offices in San Francisco in the same building as the German and Japanese consulates. Still, this might be pure coincidence and reflected nothing against Mrs. Dickinson.

They learned that Velvalee had once worked as a bank clerk. She had also been employed by the California Fruit Growers Association. Both employers gave excellent reports of her.

For a time she and her husband lived in Imperial Valley, in the heart of the Japanese colony. Mrs. Dickinson had a shrewd business head and for several years handled brokerage accounts for Japanese-Americans. Among her customers were Japanese naval officers, but this was all before the Japanese attack on Pearl Harbor and could not be looked upon as necessarily suspicious. During the last years of her husband's life, Mr. Dickinson was subject to heart attacks which cost large amounts of money. But his wife seemed to have managed very well.

Widowed, Mrs. Dickinson moved to New York. During the Christmas season of 1937 she took a job in the doll department of Bloomingdale's department store. The next year she opened her own exclusive store on Madison Avenue. There she made a great deal of money, for customers flocked to the store.

Sometimes Velvalee would mention her personal unhappiness. "Since my husband's death, life means nothing to me," she would say. She was a frail little woman who tried hard to be brave. Her customers thought highly of her. They were certain she would never try to sell them any forgeries or poor merchandise.

Velvalee often went on business trips, sometimes as far as the West Coast to see her movie-star customers in Hollywood.

The F.B.I. watched and waited for several weeks. Then their suspicions were aroused. Tucked into the well-packed boxes mailed to distant collectors, little notes were discovered among the tissue paper. To be sure, the messages spoke of dolls, but they were worded in a sort of baby talk, which might be fitting for the doll trade—or it also might be a code!

In the meantime, Velvalee had begun to feel uncomfortable. Strange customers were coming into her shop asking questions that showed they didn't know the difference between a French and a German doll. Something was wrong. It was months since she had received orders from her chief. No letters from Buenos Aires—what would happen if her friends in Argentina had been arrested? What would happen if her letter to the de Molinali woman fell into wrong hands?

Velvalee's nights were filled with bad dreams, although she tried to stay calm. Everything had been so carefully planned there could be no possible danger. If the Argentina letter failed to reach the South American agent, it would probably be destroyed there. Those Latin American countries certainly would not bother with an unclaimed letter. And if the letter had been questioned by the censor, the authorities would arrest "that dull woman" in Springfield, Ohio.

But Velvalee's troubled dreams still bothered her. She reasoned that if something had gone wrong she would have been arrested long ago. Nevertheless, there were those men who kept dropping into the shop. What were they after? Panic overcame her.

These men must be spies from competing shops, she decided. There was a New England dealer from whom she had snatched several Hollywood customers. Maybe he was behind it all. He was a trouble-maker, anyway, who had accused her of forging some of her antique dolls and tampering with the costumes. He knew a thing or two, and he was right about what she did, but the collectors never knew the difference. She sold her dolls, both the authentic and the fake, at good prices. The trade brought her money, but she was still far from her $100,000 mark. She had to go on.

Still she could not sleep. Once she left her bed in the middle of the night, put on a housecoat and slippers and went to the kitchen for a cup of coffee. She read the evening paper and studied the stock market section. Her stocks were up again. That was a comfort. As she drank her coffee, a plan grew in her mind.

Alma, her sales assistant, could be left in charge of the shop. She herself would go to the West Coast. If anything happened while she was gone, if the F.B.I. made a raid on the store, she would be informed and would not come back. She would tell Alma she was going to Florida or Canada. Time was all she needed. Time solves many problems. She had to see a former Japanese naval officer now hiding in Portland, Oregon, who would help her. If anything went wrong she'd go to Mexico, and from there to a place where a Japanese submarine would pick her up. But all this was only in her imagination, she told herself. Nothing had happened so far, and nothing would happen.

It was early morning when she finally fell asleep. Even then she awoke in a sweat of fear from a horrible nightmare. As she dressed, she decided she would not take any luggage with her on the trip—in case she was really being shadowed.

She took a taxi to the doll shop. Alma was already there. Mrs. Dickinson sent the girl out to cash a large check to run the shop for a few weeks. She said good-bye and told Alma that her brother would look in from time to time, to help her if necessary. She posted a note to her brother and entered a taxi at Madison Avenue. Glancing around, she saw a car following her.

What was it? Was she discovered after all? Once more she tried to laugh away her fears. There were hundreds of cars on Madison Avenue. But she would take no chances. She told the driver to take her to Saks at 34th Street. This department store has an overhead bridge which leads to another large store, Gimbel's. In this maze of floors and exits, no one could follow her. She lost herself in the crowd, passed over to Gimbel's and went down into the basement which connects with the subway. Through it she went on to the Pennsylvania Railroad Station. She thought she noticed a man who looked suspicious, but by now all men looked suspicious and evil. Her nerves were giving way. Without stopping to buy a ticket she went through the gate and boarded the next outgoing train bound for Philadelphia. She paid her fare to the conductor and decided to go on to Chicago and then to Portland, Oregon.

She reached Portland and went immediately to a Chinese restaurant where her contact man worked. Her heart sank. There in the window, between two posts of cactus plants, was the sign, "CLOSED." Ruin stared her in the face. There was a slim chance that she might meet some other contact man in California, but most of her Japanese friends had been moved from the coast and put in camps inland. The long journey had been for nothing.

Several weeks later she was back in New York. She still clung to the hope that the F.B.I. was not on her track. If she had been discovered, certainly it would have been all over long ago.

But Velvalee was wrong. While she tried to compose herself, the F.B.I. kept remorselessly on her trail. Three more letters had caught the eye of the postal censors. These mentioned colonial and French dolls. The letters were not signed by Mrs. Dickinson or by Mary Wallace, but with the names of other patrons of the Dickinson doll shop.

Six F.B.I. men got busy tracing the source of the letter paper. They also found the typewriters on which the letters were written. The typewriters proved to be the property of three hotels, one in Chicago, one in San Francisco and one in Los Angeles.

Mrs. Dickinson had been mistaken when she thought her excursion through the department stores had shaken the F.B.I. agents off her track. They had shadowed her constantly from city to city. They also had evidence of her overnight stops at each of the hotels from which the doll letters had been written. The letters to South America had the same typing and spelling errors of the Mary Wallace letter. The messages sounded desperate. The writer asked for money and "answers." Velvalee was cut off from the rest of the gang, and was crying for help.

Agent B's hunch had been amazingly correct. The Irish dolls mentioned in the first letter had, indeed, referred to warships. The dealer in rare dolls was one of Japan's most dangerous women spies in the United States.

The F.B.I. prolonged the term of waiting. They hoped to catch her helpers and to warn the South American governments of the true contents of Velvalee's doll boxes.

Mrs. Dickinson was later arrested when she paid a visit to her safe deposit box in a New York bank. The box contained eighteen thousand dollars in cash. She had been keeping the money on hand in case she needed it for a quick getaway. The F.B.I. agents followed her into the vault. There they announced her arrest and took away the espionage funds. The wiry little widow struggled like an angry kitten; scratching and squirming, she tried to escape.

Mrs. Dickinson was jailed as a Japanese spy. Before the trial more money and valuables were found, amounting to forty thousand dollars. This sum was about the amount she owed the U.S. Treasury in unpaid taxes. Other accounts were taken also. Her earnings from espionage were estimated at sixty thousand dollars.

She came up for trial in July, 1944, the first case of an American woman facing a possible death penalty for espionage. She wore the same clothes as when arrested, a trim brown tweed coat and a little blue hat. Six months in the Woman's House of Detention had not improved her appearance. She was pale and nervous.

Her attorney played for time. Hoping to secure a postponement of the trial until the end of the war, he claimed Velvalee had fallen ill. But the court doctor said her heart condition was normal and she had gained twenty-five pounds during her imprisonment.

The district attorney summed up his case. He told how the doll shop on Madison Avenue had functioned as an excellent front for espionage. Mrs. Dickinson had contact with Japanese naval officers. As evidence there were four code letters in her doll language. "The dolls talked," said the D.A., "and we finally learned to understand their language."

Mrs. Dickinson was not cooperative. She resented being fingerprinted and hid her face from photographers. In her high-pitched voice she explained, pleaded, lied and begged. Faced by the evidence, she knew it was hopeless to say she was innocent, but she tried to convince the court that the information had been of little value. She admitted she violated postal censorship regulations, but said her information did not endanger the United States. She had been a spy for money only.

"All my savings," she said, "had gone during my husband's illness. I was aging and I was alone. I was afraid of the future. I was so sure that I would never be found out." She believed using her customer's names was a safe blind. She also believed that her clever code could not be broken. Had it not been for the hunch of one Washington agent, she might have put over the perfect crime. But one little detail went wrong. The Japanese agent in Argentina had been removed, and Mrs. Dickinson was not informed. This one slip delivered her into the hands of the F.B.I. and sent her to prison for ten years.

Velvalee Dickinson was released in 1952 and now works under an assumed name as a nurse's aid in an eastern hospital.

CHAPTER SEVENTEEN

The Submarine Murder in Florida

The lush palm-fringed coast of Florida was one of the most vulnerable areas in American defense during World War II. The relatively narrow peninsula stretches down into the blue Caribbean Sea. Below is a chain of stepping-stone islands arching to South America. Not only did German submarines cruise the Floridian east shores but they were able to land their saboteurs on the sandy beaches in isolated coves and river inlets. Roving like hungry sharks, the Nazi U-boats torpedoed U. S. ships on their way to the ports of the Caribbean and Latin America. At times the marauders were so confident they blew up freighters within sight of Florida citizens. Many lend-lease ships disappeared below the waves to join the sunken sloops and pirate treasures of Henry Morgan and Blackbeard.

Army and Navy Intelligence were baffled. How could these daring attacks be so successfully carried out? Hundreds of patrol planes took to the air, scouring the sea for the dark wavering silhouette of a submarine or its tiny periscope cutting through the water. Report? Negative. Worried staff meetings were called at Camp Boca Ratan and Camp Murphy, but the results were only more frenzied speculations. Ship after ship added its name to the growing list of casualties until at last nearly every third U. S. vessel that churned her way into the Caribbean became a victim of an Axis attack.

There could be no doubt. A sub or fleet of subs was being refueled either on some island to the south or from Florida's own coastline. Efforts on the part of American intelligence were multiplied. Generals and admirals flew in to give their advice and consultation and left as bewildered as before.

It seemed dishearteningly apparent there was no fast solution. The intelligence officers initiated a tedious, time-consuming plan of combing Florida's bars, restaurants, cafes and nightclubs in the dim hope that someone, somewhere would make a careless remark, a slip that would provide the all-important lead. Such a task was formidable, for Florida's tourist industry has given rise to a countless number of such places and the state itself is a long one.

Many days of that spring in 1943 were consumed with intelligence officers fruitlessly following up false leads given by their contacts in the bars and restaurants, the coffee shops and dance halls.

The first break came from Palm Beach, a highly selective and elite residential community known only to millionaires. Here the social status of its inhabitants is judged primarily by the height of the elaborate walls that enclose their floriferous yards and the number of automobiles in their multiple garages. The natives of Palm Beach eschew gossip, disapprove of scandals and make something of a fetish of remaining aloof from prying eyes of the ever-present and always persistent tourists.

Pat O'Connor, the bartender at The Hurricane, gave a sideward nod to Jim Henry as an indication to sit at the far dark end of the curving bar. Jim, a plain-clothed intelligence agent, plodded methodically over the hemp flooring, squirmed onto a red leather stool and dismally surveyed the provocative figure of a semi-nude woman etched on the mirror. For the hundredth time he mused, as he waited, why people insisted on making cocktail lounges so dark in mid-afternoon that one is really only safe when guided by a seeing-eye dog. He inwardly moaned when a sailor in whites stuffed a nickel into a juke box that bubbled with red and green lights and soulfully blared out "Harbor Lights" in a slow rhythm. At the other end of the bar Pat was artistically building up a drink that looked like a rainbow filled with an assorted fruit salad. Pat put a finishing touch on his creation by adding a cherry, a dash of soda and a miniature Japanese parasol. After giving the bar a wet slosh with his towel, Pat ambled toward Jim. Leaning over his crossed arms he began his conversation both confidently and self-consciously.

"Jim, I may be all wet, wrong as a rooster, but you asked me to keep my ears open, and there was a guy in here the other day who is strictly for the birds as far as I'm concerned. Now, don't forget I may be wrong and the guy is on the square, but I just couldn't stomach some of the things he said. . . . Say? Sorry, I didn't ask you what you wanted to drink. That's a hellova note. What will it be?"

Jim grinned. "The usual, Pat. A short beer. And you can cut out all the apologies. We consider anything, including my grandmother's old book of Goethe's poems, worth following up these days. So go ahead with your story."

"Well," sniffed Pat, "this jerk was about fifty. Actually he's been coming in here off and on for sometime now and

I didn't like him the first time I seen him and he hasn't improved since. There's something about his mouth . . . sorta cruel and when he looks at you, you have the feeling he isn't really seeing you, if you get what I mean. And another thing, when he gets loaded, it don't make him happy like that guy down there. Look, he's having a ball, but not this guy I'm telling you about. He just looks madder and madder."

"Did he ever say anything to you that seemed questionable?" asked Jim.

"Well, if you want to be specific . . . no. But he sure has a bum attitude, and that's what got me to thinking. Last time he was here, yesterday, he said our secret service was all a bunch of kids, all a lot of momma's boys from Boston who couldn't find their own neckties, much less a Nazi spy. He said they were draft dodgers who like to fight the war with sharpened pencils instead of guns." Pat lowered his voice. "And it was then that he started shooting off his mouth about the submarines. 'Ship after ship,' he said, 'goes down right under their noses but the punks can't find the U-boat.' Well, Jim, you can guess I was right hot under the collar with that sort of talk, so I says, 'Just give those guys time, they'll find the lousy Krauts.' He didn't say anything, just slugged down a straight shot and grinned at me. Later on, when he asked for another drink, he'd still been thinking about what I had said because he told me that no one could beat the Nazis. He said we Americans are stupid, dumb eggheads who will be push-overs when Hitler gets here. He said we had no business being in the war in the first place and should have stayed home but now that we are, we'd better look out."

The intelligence officer lit a cigarette thoughtfully. You've got me, Pat. I can't imagine any German spy being so stupid as to talk this way in public, but he certainly is not a very cheerful soul and I think he bears a little watching. Do you have his name or where he could be found?"

"Yes, sir, I do have it." Pat was obviously delighted with the reception to his report. "His name is Charles Peters and he is the new butler for Mrs. Giffen."

Jim whistled through his teeth. "You mean THE Mrs. Giffen, the old lady who was left the estate with the lake? Getting next to her is practically impossible. But thanks a lot and keep us posted."

Jim tossed down a coin for his beer and went out into the dazzling bright light of a lowering sun.

Mr. Henry's superiors listened to his account with great interest. Mrs. Giffen was well-known in the community of Palm Beach as being a handsome woman in her sixties, a rich widow who was generous with charities, seen seldom outside the bounds of her quiet high-walled estate, and a bit of an eccentric. As the FBI pried more deeply into the affairs of Mrs. Giffen, they were unable to find anyone who had ever been entertained in her mansion nor could they trace her servant, Dietrich, who had shopped for her needs weekly before Charles Peters took over the task on a nearly daily schedule. Dietrich, it seemed, had vanished into thin air.

The next step was obvious. Someone had to get into the Giffen house for investigation. Sam Moore, a young FBI agent, working with both the Army and Navy was selected. Armed with the tools of an electrician's trade and dressed in unpressed blue overalls, Sam rang the bell of the front gate, was admitted to do a routine fire inspection and entered the servant's entrance.

Sam Moore failed to report in that night and was still absent the next morning. When no trace could be found of him or his truck, Mrs. Giffen's palatial home took on a sinister meaning.

Staff conferences were filled with problems and conflicting theories as well as strategies to combat the problem. The FBI and the Army proposed an immediate search of the estate in the hope of finding the missing investigator. The Navy, however, took a different stand. There was more at stake than a single man. If indeed, as it appeared now, the Giffen estate was a key to the Nazi submarine mystery, locating of the refueling station was more important than solving the disappearance of Sam Moore. The staff decided to wait patiently, to follow the activities of Charles Peters and to snoop about in an attempt to locate the missing FBI man and the butler, Dietrich.

The first week passed with no results. The second was no better. When the FBI pushed their wish to raid the mansion of Mrs. Giffen, Naval Intelligence again demurred with a request for more time.

While the staff and their agents sat quietly, burning with their own impatience and inadequacy, the mechanical monster of the sea increased its appetite. Two large freighters and one oil tanker were struck by torpedoes and, in the sight of land, filled the sky with flames and smoke. Additional Army and Navy Intelligence men poured into Jacksonville, Palm Beach, Havana and Miami. Shipping lanes were changed and the lend-lease program through Caribbean waters brought to a temporary halt in the face of the disastrous situation.

Secret orders from Washington, fanned by the requests

of Mr. Moore's widow, demanded immediate entrance into
the Giffen estate, but still there was the hope that new evidence would come to light to bring the case to a conclusion
without allowing a slip.

Again, it was Jim Henry who supplied important facts.

"I don't know what the exact meaning is," he told his
superiors, "but I have been trailing Peters for days now and
have seen the same occurrence repeated so often that there
must be a significance. When he comes into town he always
buys a newspaper from the same boy on the same corner.
The news kid always bawls out the headlines until Peters
approaches him, and then he says different lines. Peters says
a few words to him while getting his change. Then the boy
goes back to his headline chant."

"That sounds a bit silly," agreed Lieutenant Briggs, "but
perhaps it is some sort of hidden conversation. We cannot
afford to overlook anything. I will see that a car equipped
with a tape recorder is parked by the stand for Peters' next
trip."

Within three days, with the help of a cryptographer
flown in from Washington, it was established that the newspaper boy was delivering coded messages to the butler,
informing him of the number, time and place of ship departures. This was the needed information.

The raid of the Giffen mansion was set for the following
morning, April 26th, 1943. A small army of thirty men
made the attack in unison. The gates and doors were smashed
and a torrent of man-power, armed and determined, spread
through the many rooms of the house, filtered into the com-
plex network of basements where they uncovered a complete
submarine repair shop and a large quantity of oil drums.

In the drawing room, Jim Henry and Lt. Briggs had cornered the cowering figure of the butler, Charles Peters, who tried to delay their further advance until Mrs. Giffen could join them. Pushing past him, Jim found the mistress of the house calmly listening to a radio news report.

Tall and distinguished, Mrs. Giffen could not have been more gracious if the two men had been invited to tea. She rose, extended her hand, asked their names and gestured toward chairs.

Neither accepted her suggestion.

"You will excuse the intrusion, Mrs. Giffen," said the Lieutenant, "but there are some questions we must ask you."

"But of course. I shall be happy to tell you anything I can." She smiled.

"What do you know about the whereabouts of a German submarine?"

If Lt. Briggs had thought his abrupt question would startle Mrs. Giffen, he was wrong. She merely raised her eyebrows in a polite surprise, "Submarine? My dear lieutenant, I know nothing about a submarine. Please explain."

"Mrs. Giffen, both you and your husband were born in Germany. Is that not correct?"

"But of course. I have never made any secret of it. I am very proud to have been born a German although I am even more proud to be an American citizen now. I am like so many others who have found happiness here in this country. Young man, certainly the actions of the madman Hitler have not made you hysterically suspicious of all Germans?"

"If you will permit me, Mrs. Giffen, I would like to ask

the questions. Where is a man who was in your employment, Dietrich, your butler?"

Mrs. Giffen shrugged. "Dietrich? I do not know. At his request I let him go. I believe he wanted to join the war effort. In Ohio, I believe . . . or was it in an aviation factory in California? I cannot be sure, and I have not heard from him."

"Madam, I must ask you to permit us to search your house."

"You realize this is most irregular, but what can I do? From the noise I hear, your request comes a bit late. I believe your men are already in the process of invading my privacy." There was a definite tone of sarcasm in her voice.

"Will you please come with us, Mrs. Giffen?"

Lt. Briggs led the way into the basement where a group of men were battering down a sturdy door. As they approached, the last hinge snapped. In a well-lighted corner of a room that was otherwise filled with oil drums, Charles Peters sat before a short-wave radio sender. He was frantically calling signals. Knowing he was trapped, he reached for the gun on the desk. Three well-aimed shots from Jim Henry's gun toppled him to the cold cement floor.

With the death of her butler, all assurance seemed to drain from Mrs. Giffen. It required both Mr. Henry and the Lieutenant to assist her back to the living room.

"Perhaps you will tell us the whole story now," suggested Lt. Briggs. "It is obvious that the oil drums and the repair shop are for the Nazi submarine. Your man Peters was in touch with them through the short-wave radio. We have known for some time that your lake is connected with the ocean by a navigable river. Has your lake been the refueling base?"

Mrs. Giffen stared stubbornly ahead, never blinking.

"That is all right, Mrs. Giffen, we will pepper the lake with bombs. The Nazis will not escape this time. You will save yourself a great deal of difficulty, and perhaps gain some clemency, if you will tell us the truth."

The word clemency was attractive. The woman nodded her head miserably.

"What happened to Dietrich?" prodded the Lieutenant.

"Peters killed him. He knew too much and was uncooperative. He is buried in the cellar."

"And the electrician?"

"Peters found him snooping in the radio room. He killed him too."

"And what about the newspaper boy?"

"He delivered information to Peters. His brother works at the docks."

At this moment they were interrupted by an army aide. "Lieutenant Briggs, a radar report has just come in. A contact echo has been made with a large solid object in the middle of the lake."

"That's it. Send out a plane with bombs immediately. Our Nazi guests cannot possibly get out now. It is ebb tide and the river is too low for their escape into the sea."

In a matter of minutes, the group in Mrs. Giffen's drawing room could hear the drone of a plane as it flew low over the house and circled the lake. They counted solemnly as six bombs exploded in the water.

While Mrs. Giffen was being taken to intelligence headquarters to record the confession that put her, the newsboy,
and Peters' brother behind bars, a team of Navy divers
searched the bottom of the lake. Lying in the silt and mud
they found a small German submarine with its thin skin
crushed by the concussion of the bombs. In the debris were
also the bodies of German sailors and officers who had died
from drowning or suffocation. Some were blown to bits, and
most were unidentifiable.

Frau Giffen, who later on claimed her family tree
included not only Field Marshal Goering, but was rooted in
history amid Blücher and Charlemagne, was sentenced to
thirty years, a penalty she never carried out. She hanged
herself in a Federal prison.

The newsboy, a Florida youngster who had applied himself more diligently to the enjoyment of sunshine and outdoor
life than to his academic work, convinced the court of his
innocence on the grounds of his ignorance. He had been led
to believe, he claimed, that the jumbled sentences were part
of a radio quiz game. The text which he recited obediently
when he met Mrs. Giffen's butler was supplied by a "radio
commentator" who was later caught by British Intelligence
in Honduras where other German submarines were served
by secret Axis refueling stations.

The newsboy, Allan Percy Field, is today a respectable
newspaper publisher in a small Floridan town. He is always
more than willing to recount his unwitting part in the submarine scandal to anyone who will listen.

And so it was that World War II brought crime and
murder into the lovely backyard of one of Florida's most
dignified and celebrated residential areas.

CHAPTER EIGHTEEN

The Frogman

The cold, clammy, oily waters of Portsmouth harbor were calm that morning of April 19, 1956. A grotesque figure, clad in rubber, slipped through the sludge, never to appear again. Fate can play dirty tricks once she has buried her claws into her victim, and on this occasion her prey, resembling a Man from Mars as envisioned in a Hollywood science-fiction film, was merely a frogman serving Her Majesty's Royal British Navy.

He had left behind him the busy port with its red-bricked and white-tiled warehouses and the freighters and schooners rocking against their piers and moorings.

Swimming like an eel, the eerie dark figure, equipped with the latest underwater cameras and detection instruments, slithered toward the two Soviet destroyers which lay at anchor, the temporary floating Kremlin of the Soviet Union's chief, Nikita Krushchev and Premier Bulganin.

"This man was involved in a plot to kill our Comrades, Krushchev and Bulganin," maintain the Soviet Secret Service. Even today they claim this daring British underwater

217

swimmer intended to bring death to the dreams and lives of the two Soviet leaders. The heroic era of Communism was a part of the past. An epoch of practical men had begun. An unknown frogman, protested the Russians, carried explosives designated to blow up the two Soviet ships, taking with them their nation's chiefs.

It is a gargantuan theory indeed. But it seems improbable that a single man could ever have carried out such an intricate plan of sabotage and assassination . . . not under water.

When Commander Lionel Crabb, equipped with his flippers and oxygen tank, left the solid soil of England to plunge into the murky waters, he descended, not only into the depths of an undersea world, but into a labyrinth of world intrigue and annihilation.

The mighty Stalin had been succeeded by Krushchev and his temporary Premier Bulganin. Both attempted to charm the citizens of Great Britain. During this, their first "summit meeting," they scored. "Bulge" and "Krush," as they were dubbed immediately by the Londoners, doled out candies to the English children and were never photographed without smiles. The pictorials showed the two shaking hands with Sir Anthony Eden, having tea with the important government and labor leaders, clinking glasses with Charlie Chaplin, and as a total effect, behaving like the world's most gracious and well-groomed personages.

But, while the Soviet potentates enjoyed themselves in their roles of two Greek gods bearing the olive branch of peace, British and American Intelligence were less dignified. With audacious scheming they created a plot to disturb the pontifical aura set by the master promoters of modern Russian propaganda.

The man chosen to create the havoc was far from being an unknown secret agent. He was the world's outstanding frogman, a World War II underwater ace and hero, a knight in shining rubber armour. To his friends, colleagues and compatriots, he was affectionately known as "Crabbie."

His targets were the new Soviet cruiser *Ordzonikidze* (pronounced Our Johnny Kids Kay) and the small Soviet flotilla anchored in the Portsmouth harbor.

A year before, the *Ordzonikidze's* sister ship *Sverdlov* had docked in Plymouth and created a rousing stir among naval authorities. She was the sleekest, most modern war vessel they had ever viewed at a distance. And, at a distance they were forced to remain, for the Soviet skipper flatly refused to allow any British pilot, or personnel, to come aboard. The British stood on the wharves and shore and watched with amazement as the cruiser breezed through the crowded port, and docked with the ease and precision of a racing car.

The Western world had never seen such a ship. Indeed, the Russians had every reason to boast her radical design which gave their craft sensitive maneuverability and record speed. The experts made their guesses and naval intelligence authorities pondered the Soviet secret. Each would have given his right arm to have been able to make a blueprint of the *Sverdlov*. She must, they thought, have an entirely new hull design, auxiliary screws and several rudders.

The Soviets, who wanted to impress the West, succeeded. Furthermore, they added to the effect by keeping their secret out of reach of the Western powers.

When the *Ordzonikidze* slid now into Portsmouth with Comrades Krushchev and Bulganin on board with their doves of peace in one hand and their plot to break Great Britain away from the United States in the other, the secret service chiefs made up their minds. It was high time to have a close look at the new "tub."

The choice for the man with the radar eyes and radar mind was not a difficult one. Crabbie combined all virtues needed for such a daring project. He possessed the needed stoic calmness, was slow blooded and had proved his unselfish resoluteness. All his life Crabbie had been a dashing daredevil, eager to throw himself fearlessly into new and greater adventures. The spice of danger was his whole life and the Navy had long before deemed him to be one of those phenomena who crystallized into a being more fish than human. His friends jocosely declared he was born with fins on his feet and scales instead of hair. He was blind in his recklessness, but skillful in his tasks. During his outstanding career, Commander Lionel Crabb had fulfilled dozens of secret missions for the Admiralty and set a record by swimming two-hundred-fifty feet deep in simple, unprotected gear with a new German camera, following the movement of fishes, and surveying naval routes and underwater defenses.

One set of pictures showed the screw of a ship as it threatened to cut him in two, but and more important, the films showed the belly construction of an enemy vessel. Another pictorial sequence recorded a torpedo being shot from a submarine at a distance of only fifteen feet. Crabbie roamed the shifting sands of the sea with the same pioneering bravery that had sent the first explorers to the North Pole, or across the American plains and deserts.

Crabbie was not born on the sea. His life was filled with bumpy interludes, and often lonely, to prove others were mistaken. There were many ebb tides in his existence and many alibis for his failures.

He experimented briefly with many trades, from selling paintings in Paris to filling gas tanks in New Jersey. His peregrinations were always filled with restlessness and endless search.

When Hitler invaded Poland in 1939, thus lighting the conflagration that was to sear all Europe, Crabb wondered what he could do for England. "The mere thought of the sea is poisonous to me," he told one of his friends. "I get seasick just looking at the water in my bathtub. Guess I'm just a landlubber. Hell, I don't even know how to swim!"

Swallowing his aversion, however, Lionel volunteered for the Royal British Navy and was promptly rejected. The doctors poked and probed the skinny little five-foot-six man and pronounced him unfit for service. His tobacco-stained lungs showed a suspicion of cancer and he was almost blind in one eye.

More angered than discouraged by the rejection, Crabb joined the Navy Volunteer Reserve and, without any medical examination, was promptly sent, as a lieutenant, to Gibraltar where the former salesman was placed behind a desk doing such tedious things as making out long forms, endless reports and complicated requisition orders. He chafed under the inactivity.

On September 19, 1941, Lieutenant Crabb was growling over his assignment of requesting several hundred swagger sticks for the officers, based on the rock fortress, when a tremendous blast shattered all the windows of the office buildings.

With stunned fascination the garrison watched the scene being played in the Grand harbor below them. The Naval tanker *Denbyvale* was on fire. She quickly sank into the sea. Moments later two other tankers exploded and followed her into watery graves.

It was obvious a new underwater campaign had started. Mussolini's Italian Navy was increasing her activity and strength in the Mediterranean. Was this a submarine attack? Certainly Gibraltar had always been considered one of the world's most protected harbors. Or were the explosions the result of sabotage?

The Admiralty had to know the answer immediately. Divers descended. Within a few days they had found the information. Holes had been cut in the submarine nets — huge gaping holes made by compressed-air cutters. In addition, the frogmen found parts of a cigar-shaped, battery-powered craft, containing a sort of saddle seat for one or two people. In the front was a detachable nose-cone or warhead. This was a new type of human-propelled torpedo. Gibraltar was in danger.

If maturity ever can be traced to a single event in Commander Crabb's life, perhaps this was the time. Naval Intelligence was still locked up in a conference room to evaluate, determine and analyze the new dangers of underwater warfare, when Lionel Crabb and his friend, Bill Bailey, teamed up with three other officers and evolved a working unit of their own, called UWWP (Under Water Working Party). Crabbie was both mad and glad. His objective was simple: "I want to stop the Italian underwater attacks. It's our personal war against Mussolini."

It seemed Crabbie was overactive and underwise. But he

actually created, without knowing it, the first Allied frogmen unit in the area.

He was still unable to swim a stroke and his floating ability resembled that of a lead balloon, but what he lacked in ability, he made up for in courage, perseverance and dogged determination. His aquatic lessons lasted for hours and he was determined to lick the enemy.

The Italian underwater squads were well-trained and expertly equipped with wool-lined and silk-padded rubber suits, sturdy fins and the latest in compressed-air breathing gear, or lungs.

The British crews seemed a ludicrous lot primitively equipped. They wore their own bathing trunks, lead-weighted tennis shoes and antiquated breathing equipment. Pressures were growing. By now the Italians were developing deadlier methods; mines which clung to the hulls of British ships like lamprey eels, were detonated by timing devices. New, intricately-designed, explosives trailed in the wake of ships and, in sudden spurts of power, split the sterns of the enemy vessels.

"One day," Crabbie later told one of his friends, "I found myself embracing a cylindrical monster. A strange mine had clamped itself to the side of our ship in the region of the engine room. It was greenish in color and about three feet long. I put my ear to it and could hear the hellish telltale ticking inside. I fooled around with the firing mechanism, trying to dislocate it. Time seemed to be running against me, and I suddenly realized the clock inside might detonate the explosion chamber any second. It would be the end of the ship and everyone on board.

"I panicked and rose to the surface. 'Captain,' I yelled,

'order all hands off the ship. The engine room first.' I gulped down a slug of rum to warm me, for it was December and the Mediterranean was bitterly cold, and went back down again.

"On a second look, the mine was the most unusual type I had ever seen. I feared there could be a booby-trap which would explode if I tampered any more with the fuse section. The only solution, as I saw it, was to remove the entire mechanism from the ship's hull by cutting off the three clamps that adhered to the metal.

"The first clamp, to my joyous surprise, came off easily and the second followed in a matter of minutes. It was that bloody third one that gave the trouble. I felt the tension of knowing at any time we all might be hurled into eternity.

"Not only time, but my oxygen was running out. I surfaced for another tank. When I went down again, the over-exposure in the icy water had swollen my hands, which were scraped, cut and bruised from the work. Scratching against the iron, with the movement of the water, had sanded them raw.

"After what seemed centuries, the last clamp gave way and the mine was separated from our ship. Later, we found it was one of the most dangerous types, an ingenious affair which operated with neutral buoyancy, floating under the water at random until it was magnetically attracted to its prey."

Most of the Italian mines belonged to the pressure models. To elevate them to the surface of the sea usually meant their explosion. Knowing this, Crabbie anchored the sinister cylinder between two buoys at the same depth as he had found it and towed it away from the ship. At a safe distance, he carefully removed the detonator, thus rendering it harmless. Later, when the mine was thoroughly inspected, the clock-device inside showed the explosion would have come in a matter of seconds—twenty-three, to be exact.

Early and imperfect radar was unable to measure the speed of unidentified objects in the water and often showed large schools of fish to be submarines and vice versa. But there was a danger from strange and dangerous fish which Crabbie's outfit had to combat—human fish.

Crabb related one of these experiences to his friends after the war was over. "I remember," he said, "when I came upon a tremendous shadow in the half-darkness of forty-feet depth. It wavered closer and closer toward me, a hooded creature from the court of King Neptune.

"As it approached, I could see its goggled eyes and glaring white long hands. You guessed it. It was a well-equipped enemy Italian frogman.

"He attacked with the sharpest, most wicked looking knife I have ever seen. I drew my own to parry, and the underwater duel began. We both knew one or both of us would die. Fighting under water is a battle staged in slow motion. I am sure we were a weird spectacle, but neither of us had the mood or the time to be amused by our languorous movements and mis-aimed slashes through the murky ocean.

"My attacker's complete and scientific underwater suit was his defeat. My old bathing shorts and tennis shoes gave me more freedom and speed of motion than his heavy rubber suit and long rubber fins. I made a final plunge at him. My knife slit his suit, and big fat bubbles of air soared upward as his uniform collapsed and filled with water. He tried to reach the surface. Four days later, we fished his body out of the bay."

Thus, Lieutenant Crabb was probably the first living creature to fight a hand-to-hand commando-trained underwater duel.

He was also the first Allied naval officer to pilot a two-man enemy submarine. This product of World War II was called a "pig." Lionel and some of his men salvaged and reconstructed one from the three enemy craft which had been sunk by depth charges. The twenty-two-foot monster was put into working order and formally christened *Emily*.

"I never liked her," Crabbie told his friends, "any more than the woman for whom she was named. Each time I took her out, I went through some of the worst moments of my life. The first time, an unexpected erratic underwater current smashed her into the steel meshes of an anti-torpedo net. It nearly tore my head from my shoulders."

On his next trial run on the *Emily*, he very nearly drowned. The battery chamber was faulty and began to leak at a depth of fifty feet. "It was jolly hard to pull up from the dive," he recalled, "and I was nearly suffocated when the oxygen valve refused to open."

The third trip was the last for the *Emily*. An outside pipe broke, the tanks flooded and she nosed down to a final resting place on the shifting sea bottom. Crabb, however, wormed free from his temperamental craft and reached the safety of land.

During this time the tides of war were also shifting. Italy deserted Hitler and Mussolini in favor of the Allies.

Crabb's mission was to locate all surviving Italian-trained frogmen and work with them to detonate the mines lying in wait in the heavily populated Italian seaports. He, with the assistance of an American naval hero, Anthony S. Marsloe, a former legal advisor to Governor Tom Dewey, was commissioned to set up the Allied Navies Experimental Station in Venice.

"He was not unlike a knight out of the past," Marsloe says of Lionel. "His body belonged first to his King and then to Queen Elizabeth. This blind loyalty inspired him to overcome all obstacles. I am sure he wanted to die doing something daring."

Mussolini had been defeated. The new Italian Government sided with the Allies; loyalties and inter-dependencies switched rapidly. All Italy was suffering from the wounds of war when Crabbie discovered that his fame had spread into the camp of his former enemies. His task to recruit Italian frogmen was not difficult at all. They came to him voluntarily, eagerly and admiringly. One day the frail little Britisher confided in Marsloe, "To have a friend like you is one thing, but when your enemies respect you, that is a real honor."

A deep friendship grew between the American and the British frogman.

The Crabb-Marsloe team, assisted by their Italian frogmen officers, organized history's first and largest team of "human mine sweepers." They worked twenty-four hours around the clock to make Italy's ports free of the treacherous, death-dealing cylinders and iron-clad mines that lay in the blue waters.

Crabbie, who had wrestled in the underwater wilderness for almost five years, found himself at the end of the war hearing the applause of a British crowd who deliriously approved his war record. The man with the bad lung and the blind eye emerged from the war a hero, the world's most celebrated frogman. He was awarded the rank of commander and decorated with the seven highest combat medals, including the Order of the British Empire and the King George Medal.

The postwar world treated the war hero less kindly. The man who had established such high marks for his courage, tenacity and valiancy, no longer received such profuse accolades.

British Naval Intelligence rehired him, but only after he had experienced many ups and downs in the commercial field, including establishing a partnership in a furniture company in London.

The apparent impotence of the great Allied powers against the domination and growing strength of the USSR reactivated Crabbie's adventuresome life. As a "hobby" he took up underwater photography and produced for the Western governments some of the rarest aquatic pictures ever taken, many of which are still classified as "top secret" in the files of the various security departments.

Crabbie successfully convinced some of his naval superiors that, in his opinion, the contest between the East and the West was not only in the race for outer space, but also in the race for "underseas."

His activities were not always as a straight salaried employee of Naval Intelligence. Crabbie built his own organization and his own private unit, composed of former Navy frogmen and experienced underwater warriors, began their work for the government.

The British Navy endorsed the setup, knowing if some projects would fail and backfire, the Government officially would face embarrassment and blame.

There was a long period in 1950 when Crabbie vanished. No one saw him for months in his luxuriously decorated flat in the Knightsbridge district of London, nor did the waiters or bartenders remember serving him in his favorite hangouts.

The last time Commander Crabb visited Portsmouth harbor for his "shave and haircut" was April 17, 1956, shortly before the *Ordzonikidze* docked with comrades Kruschev and Bulganin on board. With the Britisher was a tall, bespectacled blond man, who seemed to be his friend. Together they registered at the old Sally Port Hotel in rooms apart from each other.

Neither of the two men spent much time in his hotel room. No one knows where they were during the following hours, but Crabbie was seen the same night in some of his old favorite hangout places as the Nut Bar and the Keppel's Head Hotel. He made several phone calls to his old partner in the furniture company, Mr. Maitland Pendock.

The following night, on the 18th of April, Crabbie was again seen by the waiters and bartenders of his favorite bars and restaurants.

The events which followed are unknown to the public. The Soviet Secret Service may know the details. The British and American secret services have their speculative theories, but the real and true story can only be guessed from the puzling, frightening, contradictory, provocative bits of unsure evidence and information that, like flotsam, continue to turn up on the beaches of fact.

What is known through intelligence and counterespionage is abysmal, leading only into darkness:

April 17, 1956
Crabb and friend checked in at the Sally Port Hotel.
Friend wore glasses.
Crabb around the docks.
Crabb visited bars and restaurants.
Crabb made a phone call to his partner.

April 18, 1956
The man wearing glasses who registered under the name of "Smith" checked out of the Sally Port Hotel at 3:30 p.m., paying both his and Crabb's bill.

April 19, 1956
At 10:30 a.m. Crabb phoned his business partner about a check. All further activities unknown.

April 20, 1956
Pat Rose, an attractive young lady who was very fond of Crabb, spent an impatient night waiting for Crabb, who did not arrive, nor did he phone.

On April 21, Mr. Pendock, Crabbie's business partner, began to wonder what had happened to his partner who had not been in the office since the 16th of April. Something must have gone wrong, Pendock thought, and he decided to report the matter to Scotland Yard where he was met by stony faces and, in terse words, told, "Stay out of this. You should know better than to ask questions."

The newspapers caught wind of the story and uncovered confusing facts. A certain Bernard S. Smith had bought a Danish armchair from the Pendock-Crabb Company. He paid with a personal check but had misdated it. "That's all right," Crabb had told his partner by phone at 10:30 on April 19th.

"Smith will write another check. I expect to see him in Portsmouth soon."

Naval Intelligence remained silent. M.I. 5 remained silent. Scotland Yard remained silent. Not even Crabb's mother could receive cooperation from official sources. Her son had not returned from Portsmouth.

Others of Crabb's close friends and associates took up the search. One commander went straight to the Admiralty. "Don't worry," he was told. "Crabbie will show up right enough. You must realize we are in no position to divulge any information due to the Official Secrets Act."

Marshall Pugh, a writer and close friend of Crabb's, reached the Deputy Chief of the Naval Staff. He was informed, "Commander Crabb is missing after testing some classified new equipment. There will be an official announcement very soon."

Pugh was not satisfied with such a vague, cryptic answer. "Humph," he grunted sarcastically, "and I suppose the announcement will say Crabb fell overboard during a thunderstorm."

"Oh, no," answered the Deputy Chief seriously, "this is no laughing matter. We have far too much respect for Commander Crabb to say anything so ridiculous as that."

Nine days after Crabb's disappearance, an agent of M.I. 5 Intelligence Department visited the Sally Port Hotel in Portsmouth and tore four pages from the guest registry. But it was too late to keep "Smith's" name out of the case. The papers had all reported and duly constructed their own suppositions about the man who had misdated the check for the chair.

On Sunday, April 28th, forced by the public clamor, the Admiralty issued their terse communique:

"COMMANDER CRABB DID NOT RETURN FROM A TEST DIVE. HE IS MISSING AND PRESUMABLY DROWNED."

The report went on to say the tests took place in Stokes Bay (three miles from the position of the anchored Soviet ships) and the hour was given as 10:20 in the morning.

The press still was not satisfied. How, they asked, could Crabb have been lost in a test dive at 10:20 in the morning and call his business partner at 10:30 the same day to discuss the matter of a misdated check? They voiced scepticism that Crabb made his test three miles away from the Soviet ships, and later turned up evidence that the Commander had indeed visited the *HMS Vernon,* the frogmen's training ship and a cover-up center for Naval Intelligence in Portsmouth. The *HMS Vernon* lay in the harbor only five hundred feet from the Ordzonikidze.

It took the Soviet Government a week to compose their angry two-page note to London. However, when it arrived, it was a masterpiece of stinging accusations which claimed British Naval Intelligence had ordered Commander Crabb to spy shamelessly on the new Russian ship and the activities aboard the Soviet vessel. It went on to state they had no knowledge of the whereabouts or the fate of the British frogman.

In the files of British Intelligence, there is a different set of facts which contradict the Soviet statements. During a farewell party, before the *Ordzonikidze* sped from the Portsmouth harbor, one of the Russian sailors, caught in the spirit of too much vodka mixed with Guinness stout, confided to his feminine companion, "A couple of days ago we caught one of your men." But he refused to say more, having realized he had already said too much.

Still the theories raged. What had happened to the frogman hero? Had he been electrocuted? Or speargunned? Had he been killed by Communist frogmen who discovered him while attempting to blow up the ship in order to kill Krushchev and Bulganin? Was he planting mines on the ship? Or perhaps the dive was made to discover the secret of the maneuverability of the new vessel. Did he place sound instruments? Microphones?

Whatever the unknown truth was, it seems apparent Commander Crabb was caught by the demons of destruction.

The Soviet press dived on the case like a tern after a fish. The propaganda machine went into full speed and screamed to the Communist world that Commander Crabb either spied on the Russians while they were on a friendly peace mission or still worse, had attempted an assassination plot.

Still other comrades in Moscow and Peking wove the threads of evidence into a fabric that accused the American Intelligence Service of having hired Crabb to install on the ship's hull a *sonar* system which would give the West information about the new cruiser's navigational range, through underwater sound waves. These electric spy instruments with small anchors could release themselves after a time. Had Crabb tried to attach them?

In the age of science anything is possible. Crabb could have been installing a microphone system to pick up the conversations of the crew or beamed to hear the conversation of the Soviet leaders.

In a fast answer to the Soviet note, and the unfavorable reaction of the Russian press, the British Government stated:

"The charges that the *Ordzonikidze* was spied upon are un-
true. We assume no responsibility for Commander Crabb. If
he did anything wrong, he did it on his own."

Marshall Pugh was incensed by what he felt was Govern-
mental side-stepping. "Crabb died doing his duty," he said
bitterly. "Now they are trying to make him look like a bad
boy. They are dragging his good name into the mud."

But if Crabb had been drowned in the harbor, where was
his body?

Sydney Kowles, an exfrogman and wartime buddy of
Crabbie, came to Portsmouth to search for the Commander's
remains. He was stopped at the docks by an Admiralty official.

"Don't dive. Crabb isn't down there, so just don't bother."

"Then his body has been recovered?"

"I didn't say that," was the answer. "But don't ask any
more questions. I am sworn to secrecy. But don't dive because
I would hate to see a friend of the Commander stick his neck
out when there is nothing to be gained. I know he isn't there.
Don't ask me how I know; I just do. Now go home, please."

This conversation could mean anything. Perhaps the Navy
recovered the body and kept it secret. Or Crabb was alive and
a Soviet prisoner.

On May 10th, an Admiralty officer returned some of
Crabb's belongings to his mother. They had been collected
from the Sally Port Hotel by the mysterious "Mr. Smith."

Mrs. Crabb's hopes soared. "There is one thing missing
here," she said, "that makes me know my son is still alive.
His cane is not among these things! It is really of little value

to anyone else, but Crabbie would have taken it with him—just for good luck."

Yes, some agreed, if the Commander had been captured, the Russians, out of respect for the British hero, might have permitted him to have his cane.

With the passage of time, public interest in the case died down.

Four weeks later a headless torso was fished from the harbor, but the body was too deteriorated for identification. Those who clung to the idea that Commander Crabb was killed by the Russians called the case closed.

But those who felt Crabb was still alive found new hope in a strange event that occurred some weeks after.

One morning a strange, stout woman, who spoke with a foreign accent, appeared at the Pendock furniture store. She handed a check to one of the clerks and said in a shrill voice, "Give this to Mr. Pendock and tell him to tear up the one dated 1955." By the time the astonished clerk delivered the check to Pendock, the woman had vanished. The check was signed "Bernard S. Smith."

The visit of the mysterious woman opens two more vistas of thought. It could be conceivable that British Intelligence, in an effort to close the case forever, issued a new check so that Mr. Pendock would not be tempted to pry further into the affairs of Mr. Smith.

As an alternate, the check might have been sent by Commander Crabb who was, and perhaps still is, alive. To support this possibility there is the incident of the two missing British diplomats who vanished behind the Iron Curtain and managed to send checks to their families in Switzerland as a sign of their being alive.

The British Parliament went through numerous stormy sessions on the Crabb case. At last Prime Minister Anthony Eden put his foot down on the debates by saying, "It would not be in the public interest to disclose how Commander Crabb is presumed to have met his death."

Soviet diplomats remained close-mouthed on the Crabb incident, but they frankly admit that the *Ordzonikidze* was a ship well worth an investigation. She is, they stated proudly, not only as fast, light and maneuverable as a flying fish, but also equipped with a new type of anti-magnetic armor which repels conventional mines and torpedoes. She is also equipped with new sound and radar systems and all modern sound and counter-sound detection systems. Equally radical are her built-in anti-frogmen devices which include magnetic traps.

These boasts, coming from the Russians, were verified by Finnish Intelligence after watching the maneuvers of the *Ordzonikidze* in the Gulf of Finland. The magnetic pull, according to the reports, can draw the frogmen's oxygen tanks into the magnetic field and suck them onto the hull of the warship where they are held until their life's breath is exhausted and they suffocate.

"If that was Crabbie's fate," his old friend Marsloe declared, "he was prepared for such a death. One night, many years ago, over a bottle of Italian Chianti, he said to me, 'I don't want to die with my slippers on . . . give me my flippers instead.' "

But there are still those who believe Commander Crabb is being held by the Soviets, who rescued him while he was fighting for his life pinioned on the hull of the cruiser *Ordzonikidze*.

From a very practical standpoint, it would be folly to kill a man who knows so much about British-American underwater intelligence, radar, sonar, and the specialized scientific naval advancements.

This is an opinion shared by a high-ranking French diplomat who recently returned from Moscow. He states that, during a Kremlin reception, a high government official admitted, "We have the British fish-spy."

"Do you mean Commander Crabb is still alive?"

"Sort of," the Commissar smirked. "He is Number 147 in the Lefortovo Prison. Dangerous character . . . that Crabb! He almost escaped, but was recaptured after a struggle. Now we keep him in solitary confinement. Perhaps we will put him on trial . . . perhaps not. It all depends on the British attitude. In any event, he won't be seeing London for a long, long time."

But, whatever the truth may be, Commander Crabb will not be forgotten for a long, long time either. If there is a human chance for him to return to England, he will do so. If not in this life, perhaps in another incarnation.

CHAPTER NINETEEN

The Knight in Asbestos Armor

It happened in the days before General Charles de Gaulle proclaimed the Fifth Republic. This does not imply that the events would have been automatically ruled out under the De Gaulle regime, for this spy story has a bit of the spirit of France itself. Its facts are as contemporary as the still wet painting exhibited on the Left Bank; its motives as old as the Seine herself, and its execution filled with unbelievably rare naivité. The outcome made all France laugh and raise her wine glass for the suave toast "C'est la vie."

Once upon a time, in 1950, there lived a French baron and his wife. He was as young and handsome as she was gay, lovely. And they were very rich. The baroness, petite and dark, wore her furs and jewels with exquisite grace for, being the daughter of a former French finance minister, Eleanore had grown up in the atmosphere of great elegance and the traditional French graciousness. They owned a number of sumptuous mansions, a villa on the Cap d'Antibes, elaborately appointed apartments in Paris, in addition to the regal old family estate at Bagnols-sur-Ceze where the baron enjoyed his hunting days. They moved with the weather and the flow of the best of society from Paris to North Africa, the Riviera to the country homes and back again. Neither of the two people had ever worked in their lives.

But, in spite of their wealth and position, neither was happy, especially the baron. Over the roulette tables at Monte Carlo he brooded and even the great stretch of the sapphire Cote D'Azur could not raise his spirits. Neither the best champagne nor the most carefully prepared pheasant could make him smile—for France was not what she used to be. He would angrily toss the newspapers in a heap on the floor when he read that a new government had come in on the heels of an old five-day-old one. The Glory that was France was no more. Colonies, once glad to serve under the tricolore, were now in open rebellion. France's glory had vanished. Illusive, foul-mouthed monsters called Communists wormed their way through his native country and the vexatious shadow of Stalin hovered over the productive vineyards, the long coastline, the Alps, and the people of France, his people. "Ma pauvre France—ma patrie, what has happened to you?" he cried.

A monarchist, Baron Scipion du Roure de Beruyere decided to do something for France and give up his own unemployment. A great gesture for his native land would help to calm the discomfort he felt. His sympathetic wife, Eleanore, understood, and together they searched for the one thing, the one big act that would liberate their beloved nation from the grips of the Hydra of Decadence.

In the spring of 1950, the baron and baroness drove from their palatial villa on the Cap d'Antibes to the resort town of Nice, with its slender palms that wave toward the Algerian coast. This was no pleasure trip. The baron had an objective in mind and a prearranged appointment with a Mr. Gaillard, who was obviously an enterprising man with many business talents ranging from beach concessions and open air dance halls to several loosely defined "transactions" which covered quite a gammit on the Riviera coast. In their previous telephone conversation, Gaillard had indicated a "deal" that would be suitable to both Baron Scipion du Roure's idealism and his well-filled wallet.

The baron was too interested and impressed with Gaillard's scheme to appreciate the crimson bougainvilleas that climbed the walls or the geraniums that fought unsuccessfully, red against pinks. Baron du Roure fixed his eyes on Gaillard's puffy little rosebud mouth and listened intently.

"The deal I offer you is risky, Baron," he was saying, sipping an apertif in an outdoor cafe, "but you are no man to flinch in the face of danger and you are the only man who can carry out this vitally needed plan. It will, of course, pay you well in the long run, but, being the aristocrat that you are, the loyal son of France, it will give you honor as well, which I am sure you will agree is much more important."

Du Roure's tongue held down his lower lip, a mannerism his wife had long ago learned meant he was both thrilled and excited.

"I have friends," continued Gaillard, noting, with satisfaction, the receptive attitude of his new acquaintance, "who, like yourself, are daring. You will be the final link in the long chain to thwart the Russians and to aid the last anti-Communist bastion in Europe—Franco's Spain."

The baron leaned forward. A hint of perspiration showed in his handsomely arched eyebrows.

"The answer is—uranium. We, my friends and I, are at

this very moment transporting the most valuable metal in the world out of Germany—yes, right out from under the dirty noses of the Russians—and sending it to the Franco government. This is important! We are making history! There is danger to be sure, but what is one life in times like these?"

Gaillard gave time for his statement to sink in.

"Money to you, Baron, is very little, but to our operation it has been most vital. Uranium costs us 50,000 francs per gram, but since Spain wants the metal so very badly, they pay double or triple the investment. That would give you—let's see—approximately four hundred and twenty American dollars per gram when you arrive in New York to be our top agent there—and you had ideas of emigration, anyhow!"

The baroness was way ahead of Gaillard's apparently slow mathematical calculations. She had already reached out and grasped her husband's hand to indicate her approval.

The baron was still recovering from the magnitude of the plot. There was every element he approved of and his wife's hand in his was as good as their mutual co-signature on the deal.

"I accept the arrangements."

Gaillard weaved his head in and out between his shoulder blades like a turtle and gave the open-palmed gesture of "Je ne sais pas."

"Baron du Roure, I cannot say that my friends will accept you. Of course I will do everything I can, but Alberto, Inspector Jacque Alberto of the French border police, must meet you first. No doubt I have talked too much, exposed too much already. But, *alons, chèr ami,* let us go see him at once."

Inspector Alberto's apartment in Nice was in a dark and narrow side street off the market place and barred by tightly locked doors. He was tall, blond, in his middle forties and amiably gracious. After a single complimentary remark to the baroness he began a gay, disconnected, obviously leading, conversation with the baron who was, at the same time, taking in the casually tossed Croix de Guerre medal on the end table. Underneath was another medal that appeared to be the medal of the resistance movement. Alberto looked very much like Great Britain's Prince Philip and was well aware of it.

The banter became serious. Alberto asked to be excused and took Gaillard with him into the kitchen where, through the cloth drapes separating the rooms, the baron and baroness could catch only the intermingled whispers ". . . safe . . . I swear it . . . trusted . . . patriot . . . De Gaulle follower . . . courageous . . . hates Communism . . . like . . . could be . . ."

In less than five minutes the two men returned.

"Mon ami, Gaillard tells me that you want to help our patriotic cause. As one loyal Frenchman to another I will tell you the whole story. Our operation is in connection with a military branch, backed by the Deuxiéme Bureau. The French Parliament has not voted enough funds for this very important work and therefore we must turn to private sources and patriots. To be honest, we need the staggering amount of 10,000,000 francs for the first consignment. You indicate you have such an amount and, more than that, you would be willing to help us get the uranium to Spain. For your money, I can guarantee you will have twenty thousand dollars payable in America or France."

This was it, the baron thought. He was ready to accept

once again, but before he could say, "Oui," Alberto looked sad and shook his head.

"Baron, you have no idea how much I would like to embrace you into our secret fraternity. How much I would like to kiss you on either cheek and wish you well as one of us— but alas, I cannot. Only yesterday I received word that the Soviet counterespionage agents in Germany and Spain are beginning an investigation. They may pounce on us at any minute. I regret, sir, that I must ask you to wait until you are officially cleared by our immediate chief of operations in Paris and our friends in Spain."

The baron and baroness not only agreed, but were impressed with the carefulness of the organization. They exchanged glances and furtively wagged their heads at each other.

In the end, it was agreed that more rapid expedition of matters could be done if the four were to travel to Paris to meet the chief in charge, Colonel Carlicchi, and together they spent the night at the baron's villa in order to get an early start the next morning.

The baroness saw to it that the evening was befitting their important guests. There was their finest linen, sparkling crystal, best vintage of wines, savory roast duck and dainty pastry with subtly flavored ices. While the conversation was indeed gaiety itself, there was a serious undertone nevertheless.

After their last demi-tasse and Napolean brandy, just before retiring, Du Roure challenged his guests to a shooting contest. The baron took aim at a buoy that bobbed on the moonlit sea, fired and missed his target several yards. Alberto laughed and boasted his marksmanship, the result of his vast experience as an officer in the resistance movement, but he too missed by a couple of inches. Gaillard squinted his beady little eyes, raised the carbine and sank the buoy almost without looking at it.

"C'est bon," congratulated Alberto and, turning to Du Roure, added, "Gaillard, you see, is our trigger man." They said good night and the baron went to his room to sleep with visions of victory dancing in his crew-cut head.

In Paris the next day, the baron established his new friends in the opulent apartment on Avenue Foch belonging to his mother-in-law, and waited impatiently for his introduction to the colonel. It was not long in coming.

Colonel Jean Berthier of the "Counterintelligence Department" was an impressive figure of a man. In a film, his role would perhaps be best suited for some tall, straight, handsome man such as Cary Grant or Gregory Peck. And there was no doubt as to his intelligence, for he questioned the baron as if he were a nobody-in-particular. With almost savage thoroughness he pried into Du Roure's family background, his political opinions and the part the baroness would play in the transaction. Unaccustomed to such interrogations, the two young people were at a loss as whether to be angry or impressed by his arrogant prying. Their decision fell on the latter attitude, for the scheme was too momentous to be overshadowed by anyone's mere psyche.

At last the colonel appeared to be satisfied. "Baron du Roure, it is my studied opinion that you are quite suitable for the task that lies ahead. You are permitted both to finance and to handle the first precious consignment of uranium for our brave neighbor country. If all goes well, there may be other more important—and profitable—ventures for you."

The baron expressed his deep appreciation for the confidence and pledged his life to the safety of the all-important uranium convoy. He hurried away to the Worms Bank and drew out ten million francs which he himself, not trusting his chauffeur, took to Berthier and Alberto.

At the appointed hour of nine that night, Gaillard, Alberto and Berthier rapped on the door of the Du Roure apartment and lugged in a one hundred thirty-five pound case which resembled an overgrown army footlocker. Inside was another trunk made of heavily polished wood and adorned with metal hinges and various seals. Nestling within the second case was the third and last, made of lead and carefully sealed with wax, lead wires and numerous stencilled messages: Danger. Do Not Open. Handle with extreme caution.

It was a solemn occasion when the colonel saluted the baron and handed him an envelope marked "Top Secret" and official military orders for his an Eleanore's entrance into Spanish territory.

Over a little supper comprised of such delicacies as goose liver paté, frog legs and chilled artichokes that the baroness had prepared herself, plans were laid step-by-step for the rest of the transaction. It would, obviously, take some time. The baron and baroness were to transport the case by automobile to St.-Jean-de-Luz on the Bay of Biscay where they would go into hiding until they received further orders for crossing the border where they would be met by General Rodriguez of the Generalissimo Franco's army representative. The transfer and payment would take place at that time.

With the business arrangements concluded, everyone slipped into a comfortable pattern of informal language. The baroness was called "Nelly" and Gaillard agreed affably to the baron's appellation of "Scarface." As a matter of fact, he apparently approved of it wholeheartedly. It was agreed he should travel with the Du Roures since Duclos' French Communists might, and the Soviet Secret Service might, get wind of the plot and attempt to ambush the car. A triggerman was always welcome.

With the large case carefully secured in the car, the baron and baroness began their trip to St.-Jean-de-Luz. An unfortunate case of fever had forced, to their disappointment, "Scarface" to travel by plane, but the two brave aristocratic defenders of freedom felt they could, with caution, manage by themselves. Trying not to appear furtive, they spun down the highway in their American automobile as far as Angouleme, where they registered in an out-of-the-way pension under an assumed name, little realizing their large foreign car was causing more attention than if they had stopped at a luxury hotel accustomed to such extravagances.

Their aperitifs on the veranda were interrupted by a wire from Colonel Berthier. Between the not-too-carefully cloaked words, the Du Roures read the meaning of the telegram. There would be a delay in completing the delivery of the uranium and, more frightening, the implication that Gaillard was under suspicion as to his loyalty. It was a restless night for the young couple.

Despite the magnificent June weather, the verdure of the countryside and the beauty of the sea, the Du Roure's found St.-Jean-de-Luz a nightmare. Phone calls from Paris interrupted them while they were reading wires from Paris and letters flooded them from Colonel Berthier announcing one delay on the heels of another. They fretted and fumed and each day the darkness of the intrigue hovered more closely.

Answering an urgent request to meet Alberto in Bayonne for further instructions, Eleanore and her husband were surprised to find, not the inspector, but the dashing colonel himself, surrounded by an armed escort. Berthier's face was worried and he paced back and forth in obvious deep concern.

Indicating they should be alone, the colonel led the way to the corner of a porch and told the anxious pair the bad news.

"Gaillard," he whispered, "is a traitor. He has tipped off the Russians and I fear for your well-being as well as the cause we represent. He sold out. He was a double agent."

"What is our next move, Colonel?" asked Du Roure in a low voice.

The colonel extended his heavy cigarette case, lit his own and chewed the smoke pensively. "There is nothing we can do except to be prepared and alert. First, are you armed? That is good, but in any event Alberto will be with you as an escort. Unfortunately, I will have to return immediately to Paris. You will have word from me shortly."

For the following three days the baron and baroness attempted to enjoy their mediocre hotel. Uppermost in their minds was the problem of getting the green signal for their trip into Spain. On the fourth day, a wire arrived from Paris: "It is too dangerous. The time is not right. Return to Paris."

In a whispered conference, Alberto convinced the baron and baroness that a better plan would be to cross over France to their villa on the Cap d'Antibes on the Mediterranean because, if the Communists had established roadblocks, his police card would assist them to continue their trip.

The trip to the Mediterranean villa was ghastly, a combination of nervous fear, hysteria, apprehensions and such difficulties as loose spark plugs, illusive gasoline stations, a punctured exhaust pipe and rattles that appeared from the virtual nowhere.

As a safety precaution against the penetrating rays that could possibly escape from the Pandora box in the rear of their car, the baron insisted on keeping the windows open, with the result that both he and his wife developed sneezing, dripping, nose-reddening colds. Every new turn in the road brought the fear of a Soviet roadblock. Fortunately, however, none loomed over the horizon and at three in the morning the fatigued, fraught, crochety pair reached the villa on Cap d'Antibes and fell into their respective beds only to be plagued by wild dreams of brutish men in Soviet uniforms, loud explosions, black abysses and long chases through labyrinthian passages.

Morning brought a new problem—where to hide the treasure chest until they could take it to Spain. There was radiation danger. At first they put it in a cupboard with a sturdy lock, but Baron du Roure noticed that each time he passed the door he experienced a quickening of his heartbeat and pounding pulse. It seemed to him that Eleanore was more flushed than usual and he deduced that they were being victimized by the powerful element. He ordered two asbestos vests and wore his constantly, even at night, under his silk pajamas, even though they had secretly buried the footlocker in the garden. Again, in his uneasy sleep, he dreamed the box had been found; so early the next morning it was returned to a closet on the top floor of the villa. In spite of their precautions with the asbestos vests and their new asbestos gloves, both the baron and baroness felt increasingly weak, as if their strength and good health were rapidly ebbing away.

Days were as delirious as their nights were terrifying. After a week of lugging the heavy case from spot to spot, Alberto made the feared announcement: the Russian Secret Service had located the position of the uranium by the use of highly sensitive instruments. It was absolutely imperative that the villa be surrounded by an army of guards.

The presence of this line of protectors made the baron and baroness feel more secure from the outer world, but they knew they still faced the inner dangers from the constant radiation. What an agony!

Within ten days, Du Roure and Nelly were invited to a conference over a luncheon with Colonel Berthier. Knowing their sensitive taste buds the colonel suggested the most elaborate and expensive restaurant the Champs Elysée had to offer. He had even been so thoughtful as to order the menu ahead and the chefs had prepared the "poisson en vin." The best vintage champagne was in the silver ice bucket upon their arrival.

It must be confessed that the meal was lost on the aristocratic couple because of the bad news the colonel had to share. Being a man accustomed to danger, his own appetite, however, did not appear to be impaired and he cleaned his plate each course with apparent gusto. The baron could not keep from being impressed again with the colonel's unemotional approach to misfortune and peril.

"As I feared," he was saying as he savored the amber wine, "Gaillard was a lecherous traitor. I had to have him—removed. Because of his information to the enemy, you were very nearly captured at St.-Jean-de-Luz and the transaction with General Rodriguez will have to be delayed. While on the surface this may look like a great tragedy, I believe we can call it a blessing in disguise. We will turn the tide of adversity into a sea of victory and profit."

The baron played nervously with the silver before him and held his lower lip down with his tongue.

"This delay," continued Berthier, "will give us time to amass more uranium and to move it all in with one trip. Any child can see the value of a single crossing over the border instead of several. I told you when we first met that if all went well the first time, you would have more opportunities, but this was on the side of caution because, quite frankly, I wanted to test your bravery and reliability. I am now sure that you both are remarkable people who can be trusted. You have proved yourselves admirably in the face of danger."

The baroness reached out and patted her husband's well-manicured hand.

"What do you want us to do?" asked Du Roure.

"It is very simply a matter of money. Bring me another five million francs and I will see that the shipments come into your hands."

The baron looked a trifle stunned but tried not to show it before the colonel. Making a silent inventory of his cash funds, he was forced to make an admission that they did not have such a large amount at their fingertips right at the moment.

While the colonel frowned and was plainly upset with this news, the baron had a brilliant idea.

"Eleanore has a magnificent diamond necklace given her by her father. It has been appraised between fifty-five to sixty-five million francs. I can get it from my vault if you would be willing to accept it as collateral. Perhaps you could borrow enough to finance the additional shipments."

The colonel did not hesitate. "But, of course, that will do very nicely. And you, Eleanore, in the spirit of the true French patriot, are momentarily sacrificing your own gems for our great cause. Vive la France!"

Eleanore shrugged that it was nothing.

The colonel made a weak gesture to pay the check but graciously demurred at the baron's insistence.

The necklace was delivered to the colonel and the Du Roures returned to their villa and once again donned their asbestos vests although each confided that the trip had had salubrious physical effects.

During the following week the colonel visited their fellow-conspirators at the villa. His luggage included another four cases of uranium and a large glass cask, wicker-wrapped and marked "made in Italy" which Berthier explained was most definitely a victory, for it contained "heavy water." As soon as the world tensions over the Korean war simmered down a bit, they would be ready to execute one of the greatest coups of the century.

On the terrace, beyond the ear-shot of any servants, the colonel explained the financial statement to date. The necklace had brought only thirty million francs but he was sure the baron would be only too happy to supply the missing twenty million. In reply, the baron confessed he was a bit short in his French accounts but could scrape up a few million francs and make up the rest in Swiss gold and American dollars.

This was agreeable to the very kind and understanding colonel but he added that the money should be not too long in coming for he was personally needed in Spain to make further arrangements for a delivery of such value and magnitude.

The next day the colonel left, ostensibly headed toward Franco-land, leaving the Du Roures in the capable hands of Alberto.

The last days of summer fluttered by. Alberto was everpresent to assist in the moving of the cases and the jug of heavy water. He brought news from Nice and encouragement on the project. Chafing under the yoke of danger and delay, the baron suffered untold miseries which only Alberto could allay. Alberto was not only a capable bodyguard but he also understood the problem that the baron had a great deal of money tied up in these boxes and was eager to get them into the proper hands. Alberto also appreciated the baron's newly found talents and capacities, a natural for the exciting world of shadows, cloaks, daggers, intrigues and beautiful women who smoked Turkish cigarettes from long ebony holders. Alberto helped the baron write lengthy letters to the "European Military School of Counterespionage" as well as flower-phrased letters to leading American and English generals, an assorted group of United States senators and some other high-ranking officials in secret capacities all over the free world. Well-informed and cooperative, Alberto supplied the names, addressed the envelopes and posted the letters in Nice himself.

While these activities occupied the baron for some time,

it did not completely answer his need for a conclusion to the operation. Fearing the baron was on the verge of cracking under the strain, Alberto urged a conference with Colonel Berthier. Together they hatched a new scheme, one with the color of the Arabian nights and a piquant dash of something they had read in T. E. Lawrence's memoires.

The pale grey of twilight was just enclosing the villa when a figure clothed in flowing robes and burnoose leapt agilely up the marble steps to renew his acquaintance with the baron and his wife. He had previously been introduced by Alberto as the purchasing agent for the New Israeli army so the baron escorted his bearded narrow-eyed acquaintance into the drawing room.

Bowing low and offering a rapid forehead to heart salutation, the Arab came directly to his point. He was not, he said, connected with the Israeli or Egyptian government. Only a fool such as Alberto could be so hoodwinked. He was a Soviet agent equipped with power and money to do business with the baron. For the first shipment of uranium alone he had been instructed to offer three hundred and sixty million francs which was, it had to be admitted, a better deal than what Franco or the U.S.A. could offer.

Baron du Roure was not to be swayed by the offer of mere money. His mission in life was greater than franc notes. He promptly threw the invader out and dashed to the telephone to call Colonel Berthier in Nice as had been prearranged in the event of just such an emergency.

In Nice, Colonel Berthier and Alberto were having another round of Pernod in a small bistro in a dark alley when the "Arab" joined them. From the table where they sat with their heads together, occasional phrases of laughter floated into the smoke-filled bar room. After allowing enough time for Du Roure to make his phone call, Alberto and Colonel Berthier left for the baron's villa, where they scowled and feigned worry over these new international complications.

They questioned the baron in detail about the appearance and distinguishing marks of identification of Du Roure's swarthy visitor.

"Alberto," concluded the colonel, "this dangerous agent must be stopped. It is up to you. He might have to be killed or the Russians will assassinate you." Together they departed, leaving the baron to sink into a state of nervous exhaustion.

Later that night, Alberto's Mercedes whined up the drive and skidded to a stop in front of the villa. The colonel leaped from the car, summoned Du Roure and pushed him into the car. In silence they drove to a lonely stretch of sand where, by the light of the colonel's flashlight, Du Roure identified the inert body wrapped in flowing robes and laying face down on the beach. Blood and bullet holes showed on the Arab's back. A Soviet spy had been eliminated.

Du Roure felt ill, but was reassured by the strength of Colonel Berthier. "He was far too dangerous to be allowed to live! Alberto, see that the boys take care of the body. It must never be found."

As the Mercedes slipped into the night back in the direction of Cap d'Antibes, the prone figure crawled to his knees, shook the sand from his hands, discarded his blood-smeared costume and began his long hike back into Nice.

If there had ever been any doubts in the mind of the baron, they were now completely erased. The colonel and Alberto were so serious about protecting the uranium they were will-

ing to kill for its safety and, as Du Roure pointed out to Eleanore, while all their money was tied up in the cases, at least
the precious boxes were in his own keeping. It was, then, absolutely imperative that they remain in his possession and this
meant the balance of the payment would have to be met. One
could not afford to lose the bulk of the fortune because of a
trifling debt to the colonel. By scraping the bottom of the family coffer, the rest of the money was delivered and the uranium
became the official property of the baron and baroness.

The weeks became months, and the two young people continued their vigil over their precious possessions. During the
time, many other exciting events happened. For instance, there
was the time when some Soviet agents stole the plans of a new
French jet. Du Roure was invited to aid counterintelligence
by supplying the small total of thirty million frances, a mere
eighty-five thousand dollars.

As a reward for this monetary service, the colonel promised Du Roure the fulfillment of the baron's greatest wish in
life—the Legion of Honor. Berthier had hit a vital point. Du
Roure, nobly born and rich, considered this the ultimate
acquisition. He filled out all the many papers and scraped
together the money needed to track down the culprits who held
the important blueprints.

Both time and ideas were running out for the colonel and
Alberto. But they could not resist the temptation of further
milking their innocent prey, despite the fact the baron showed
some nervousness over the rumors that became increasingly
persistent that he was being the fall-guy for a big swindle.
Even an old friend of the family, a lawyer, brought the same
story to him. Whenever Du Roure appeared edgy and suspicious, Alberto and Berthier would take a long trip and lay

low until they had dreamed up another scheme. The second shipment of uranium was now cached in the Paris Military Academy according to the plans of Alberto, but the large case was still in their own safe keeping in the garden at the foot of a marble copy of the statue of Victory.

For some time it had been evident that the transaction with Spain was off, but Colonel Berthier's brother, an FBI man in Washington, was working out an even more profitable deal for Du Roure.

During one of Alberto's prolonged absences around Easter time, Eleanore and her husband decided to do some investigation on their own. They drove to Marseilles where Alberto had said his family lived. There they found not Alberto, but his handsome wife, ruling regally over a newly furnished elaborate bar.

But the Du Roures had no time to smell a rat, for Alberto showed up with his usual clairvoyant sense of timing and his usual masterful explanation. He, their loyal servant and steadfast friend, had suffered the agonies of hell for their cause, he said; had been kidnapped at the Marseilles railway station by Russian goons, drugged and driven to Berlin where he was cast into a filthy, lice-infested cell and left to languish except for the many horrible hours when he was brutally interrogated by his merciless enemies about the location of the uranium.

Alberto showed welts and bruises on his legs and back and inferred that far worse things had been perpetrated which, out of deference to the gentle baroness, he would not divulge. Finally, after repeated sessions under the lash of the tribunal, the Red inquisitors were defeated by his physical stamina and moral intrepidness and reluctantly released him.

Alberto was pleased with the reception to his story, for the baron's eyes filled with tears and Eleanore wept openly. For the next week he was treated with solicitous kindness and nursed back to health at the villa.

Finally, at the end of eighteen months since the advent of the hoax, a swordlike stab of painful suspicions penetrated the baron's trusting mind. Could it be that Alberto and the colonel had stolen the uranium from the French army and deposited it with him as a ruse? Perhaps, he decided, it would be wise to face the colonel with the facts as he saw them and to demand the return of the necklace, to see what the colonel would say.

Trundling the uranium with them to Paris, the baron and baroness sought out their handsome friend.

Colonel Berthier was his usual understanding and sympathetic self. He invited them to dinner and listened solemnly.

"But, of course, I understand your impatience, for I have been sick with the delay myself. And, as for the necklace, my dear madame, you must have it back, not only because it is very beautiful and very valuable, but also because of its sentimental value. It will be very easy to retrieve it, for it is in the safe keeping of a notary in Dijon. He will release it for only five million, five hundred thousand francs."

Delighted with the colonel's unblemished frankness and sincere willingness to return the jewels, the baron shelled out the money.

Colonel Berthier was beginning to weary of the game of dupe. While the baron's credulity was far from depleted, his bank account was. The goose was running out of golden eggs. The only possibility appeared to be to stall the baron, and to do this he created a new character on the scene.

The baron was introduced to the "chief," the brains behind the hazardous operation, General Combaluzier, who had at random selected his name from the metal plate that labels the manufacture of France's most popular elevator.

The general was as solid and confident as the colonel was brilliant and clever, and the two men had the same flair for fabricating fantastic stories on the spur of the moment. He expressed his faith and gratitude to the Du Roures for their sterling qualities and unfailing devotion.

Hanging onto the lapel of his suit in a manner he had affected from the famous Churchill posture, he strode up and down the room with his chin leading and droned on sonorously:

"I am so very happy Colonel Berthier has brought you two brilliant young people here to see me. I have wanted to meet you for a long time, but I am sure you will understand how busy I am with so many details, so many agents, so much to think about. I feel I can confide in you that the affair of the uranium is going along quite well. It is true, events have not moved as rapidly as I would want — and as you have wanted, but it will be to our advantage in the long run and I can assure you that our V-day will be the first of January.

Yes, we will begin the New Year with the uranium in the proper hands and a neat profit in your hands. What could be a better present for 1952?

"And Baron Scipion du Roure, on that day I will salute you for another reason. January first is to be the day that you will be officially announced as the noble recipient of the

Legion of Honor. Here, let me pour you, dear baron, a glass of wine and may the three of us drink in advance to that memorable occasion which you so greatly deserve . . ."

The general poured the wine, made the toast, and saluted the baron. He then bowed over the hand of the baroness and kissed it in gingerly but gently.

Everyone shook himself from the solemnity of the announcement, and the baron tried to look as if he had worn the decoration in his button-hole all his life.

Seeing the stage was still all his, the general continued, "The other things I have to tell you are simply secondary, an outgrowth of all the rest, but perhaps you will be interested to know that there are certain powerful and wise French officials in high ranking positions who have kept an eye on you during these times. You are, Baron du Roure, in the position of being invited, *oui*, even requested, for some very important diplomatic posts. Here, for instance, are letters from the United States Department of State which I now have the pleasure of showing you because I know they will be treated in greatest confidence by you both."

The ink on the papers was scarcely dry, but the baron read the complimentary letter and his heart swelled with pride.

Before the baron and the baroness left Paris, they paid a call on his mother-in-law, Madame Patenotre. They were quite frank that they were without funds, had sold the Cap d'Antibes villa, the American car, drawn out their funds in Switzerland, rented their apartments and mortgaged the old family estate. They were equally frank in saying they had not lost their money in any such silly way as gambling. Their sincerity was irreproachable and convincing. Madame Patenotre gave the young couple money to tide them over until the first of the year.

New Year's Eve was a frightening mixture of emotions for the baron and Eleanore. One moment he felt like the trackman on the last lap and each glass of champagne boosted him into a state of exhaustion. The next moment, glazed eyed he peered at his best friend at the party and expected him to draw a gun. Tomorrow would be his ultimate day, but this must not be his last night. There were times during the evening when he felt his taut nerves acting like a garrot and other seconds when the sense of the coming victory transcended everything except his own success and his love of Eleanore.

Their servant wakened them, as usual, with trays of coffee, juice, croissants and large pats of fresh butter. As usual there were the flowers and the newspapers. Outside there was the usual winter grey sky as a backdrop to the ragged skyline of Paris.

And as usual there was only the impersonal news of names neither of the Du Roures knew outside of a small social circle. They both frantically ran their fingers down the list of those promoted to the rank of Legion of Honor. There was no mention of Du Roure. Eleanore sat on the side of her husband's bed and stroked his hand. She later picked up the newspaper he flung against the wall and listened helplessly while he called his lawyer.

Four days later, the baron produced his own deck of cards and played them hard. The general appeared in answer to his request, armed with a large box of candies for the baroness. The baron asked many questions which were answered casually by the general. Everything was still in order although, God knew, it was difficult during these times to find people who would carry out details. The diamond necklace was on its way to the baroness; the omission on the name of Du Roure from the roster of the Legion of Honor would be rectified with apologies from the newspaper and the colonel was on his way back from the United States with more money than had ever been dreamed of.

On his departure, the general slapped Du Roure on the back and bowed over the baroness' hand. He was followed down the stairs by two police officers who had strained their ears through the crack in the bathroom door and two more stationed in the hall.

The dragon had been beheaded.

The police came to pick up the uranium and cautiously, layer by layer, hinge by hinge, wire by wire and testing all the time with their geiger counters, finally disclosed the diabolical contents—sand from the beach of Nice, weighted with "heavy water" from the Mediterranean and fused by a large lead pipe.

This was the end of the Pandora box which, had the baron dared to open sooner, would have saved, rather than given, the many troubles. The total fee for his purchase was approximately a third of a million dollars and the distance the case had traveled from rooms to garden, garden to rooms plus various trips into Paris amounted to considerable mileage.

The trial in Paris brought forth the true identities behind the masks. Colonel Berthier turned out to be Carlicchi who held a previous record for petty theft in 1947. The Churchillian general was no other than Gagliardone, an artist in black-marketeering who had served a term at hard labor for stealing and fencing stolen goods. Alberto was a local man of Nice, an ex-gendarmes dropped from the force for certain "irregularities." Gaillard, thought dead but very much alive, was the nearest to playing a straight role, a man with a quick eye for easy money. He was not brought to trial.

France, the home of the true farce, laughed its way through the trial. Everyone, from the judge to the accused, had their moments of witticism.

Judge, speaking to Alberto: "Have you ever before been convicted of a crime?"

Alberto: "During the occupation—oui."

Judge: "Ah hah! For resistance?"

Alberto: "I got caught with a blackmarket ham."

Judge: "Mais that was only *plat de resistance!*"

And when General Combaluzier took the stand, the judge asked his real name and then inquired about the reason for his selection of this particular alias. Cagliardone, pouted and thought before explaining that he "had to have some name and was riding on an elevator at the time."

The four knaves stuck together. They twinkled at each other during the sessions and showed no remorse for what had been a lucrative lark. They could not, and probably honestly, state what had happened to the money. "It went very quickly — a little here — a little there. A gift for the baroness or a bottle of the best brandy for the baron."

Alberto and Berthier were found guilty of wearing illegal uniforms and decorations, abuse of confidence and swindling. The penalty: four years imprisonment. The general, a newcomer in the drama, was sentenced to only eighteen months.

Gaillard, the one partner in crime free to talk about the incident, was only too eager, and he had his own definite views of the case. "I really believe," he used to say, "that Baron du Roure shouldn't have let the boys down like that. After all, he had a lot of fun playing the secret agent and spy and we provided him with all the props like uranium and heavy water and the Soviet, East German, Arab and American Secret Services. Sure, it did cost him a little money, but what doesn't cost these days?"

CHAPTER TWENTY

Francis G. Powers, Modern Space Spy

Under clear, blue, sunny skies the soldiers in Major Mihail Voronov's Ural Command relaxed. They had every reason to claim a vacation after the weeks of arduous drills and difficult maneuvers.

In addition, it seemed the entire world was looking for peace. Comrade Nikita Khrushchev was to celebrate the First of May in Moscow in accordance with the respect due the Soviet revolution. At that very moment he was preparing to fly with his entourage of commissars, secretaries, interpreters, secret service personnel to Paris for the summit meeting.

Russia's reigning dictator was scheduled to sit down with General de Gaulle of France, President Eisenhower of the United States and Prime Minister Macmillan of the United Kingdom.

This was a great moment. Tensions could be reduced and co-existence between the Soviet dictatorship and the free world would be discussed. It was agreed in the hearts and minds of serious thinking men that this historic meeting in the spring of 1960 could wipe out the fears of atomic war.

Then it happened: an historic event which shook the world and broke up the summit meeting in Paris.

Major Voronov's men had captured the first American space spy.

Far away, the Soviet radar screens saw their first blip, an unidentified object. A cloud . . . a Russian plane . . . a mistake in their own instruments . . .

Dials spun; buttons were pushed. Air alerts sped along the Soviet air defense network. "This is not a flying saucer," said Major Voronov. "This is a foreign plane. The pilot knows he has been discovered. Watch . . . watch . . . he is zig-zagging. He is trying to change his course. Yes, see, he is trying a long circle around our rocket launching base. Get him into your range. Fire!"

One American pilot tried to outwit the Soviet air defense system.

Frances G. Powers stood a slim chance.

From Pakistan to Norway, traveling at 65,000 feet in his bullet-like jet, Captain Powers' plane was no more than a dust mark on the tracking scope.

A rocket blasted out, gathering momentum and speed as it broke away from earth.

Voronov peered into the screen. Two specks headed toward each other.

Then the screen was filled with confusion.

"We hit the target."

Major Voronov ran into the sunlight and focused his binoculars on the sky. The sunlight glinted on bits of the metal. Then there was a small figure mushrooming down in a parachute.

Frances Gary Powers was captured by Voronov's men of the Soviet authorities. His U-2 aircraft had penetrated the USSR and flew 1200 miles over the heart of the Russian missile-launching area. Reputable sources say that his was the forty-eighth plane sent by the United States on reconnaissance missions in a period of four years.

With Powers in prison, Russia's Khrushchev glowered on his arrival in Paris. The clown-like little man raised his fist and demanded Power's life as a spy. The United States, he added, was entirely to blame for an aggressive and unfriendly act of espionage. The world shuddered. What was to have been a peaceful summit meeting dissolved into a vat of nitroglycerin!

President Eisenhower laid the cards on the table. Yes, he said, the United States has organized space espionage because it is the only way to protect the fifty states and the free world against surprise attacks from behind the Iron Curtain. Since Soviet dictators decline the idea of aerial inspections for all nations by the United Nations, sky-spying is the only form of self-protection the United States possessed.

The President of the United States defended Francis G. Powers' actions.

The Soviet Union has woven a network of spies through the free world. Through the activities of the Rosenbergs, the first atom bomb secrets were sent into Russia.

But space espionage is new.

A new breed of spies has invaded outer space. These are not only pilots, astronauts, analysts, technicians . . . the human animal ... but mechanical espionage agents which see, listen, remember and talk to only those who understand their strange language.

World-wide, globe-girdling spy networks of electronic equipment have been installed . . . the missiles, the anti-missiles, and the anti-anti-missiles, to name but a few. All major powers pride themselves on a fence of giant radar screens to combat counterespionage in the air. There are "sniffer" aircraft which take photographs and air samples, picket submarines, balloons bearing radios and cameras, radio ears which make tape recordings anywhere in space—and hear everything.

In the electronic world, the masters over the spy-organizers are the "brains" and the "computers" which digest and analyze all space reports. The "eye in the sky" can photograph any area on earth and transmit it through television to us earthlings.

The first hint of the use of aerial espionage came in 1917 when French, German and United States planes buzzed back and forth over the front lines gathering information about numbers and movements of troops.

A later, and unique case, developed when Hitler was in power. The Nazi Secret Service was baffled by a sky-writer who spread his trail of smoke across the sky, advertising soft drinks. When this story was unravelled, it was discovered the pilot was giving coded trip-offs concerned with German troop movements. A French spy in Berlin then informed his intelligence chief in Paris of planned troop military movements.

The Nazis themselves used air spies over Iceland and Greenland. Using the excuse that the planes were gathering weather data, a fleet of aircraft operated for over two years until they were destroyed by an American naval expedition, aided by the courageous Danish and Norwegian sky patrols.

Göring's Luftwaffe officers photographed large sections of the British Isles in order to "blitz" them with greater accuracy. The United States air-raid attacks on Berlin brought back aerial photographs of the secret V-2 rocket launching sites of Peenemunde which were later wiped out.

The United States Consul in Gothenburg, Sweden, William C. Corcoran, learned of the secret Peenemunde base and suggested the photographic attack, thus helping to save London.

To combat the growing strength of aerial espionage, the Nazis developed counterespionage methods, camouflage, to confuse the pilots and bombadiers. As one example, the Germans built a make-believe river through Hamburg. Thinking it to be the Alster, American airmen misdirected their bombs for a considerable time. Aircraft factories, train stations and strategic areas were also painted and disguised in the United States.

A forerunner, radio spying is closely akin to space espionage. The OGPU operated some fifty secret radio stations in France, Nazi Germany and Belgium during World War II. Important information·was relayed directly to Moscow.

Just as modern radios have been developed, specialized cameras are now so advanced that two jet planes can photograph a strip of the globe five hundred miles wide and more than twenty-five miles long in a single shot. Francis G. Powers was in the process of photographing only a small section of the vast USSR when he was shot down and exposed as a space spy by two bits of evidence: pictures and a poison needle meant for his own suicide.

The range of feats a modern spy camera can perform is impressive. Jet planes can fly day or night through good weather or bad, using infrared devices from heights as high as fourteen miles. The aerial photographers can take pictures of anything they wish . . . the Kremlin, airfields, airstrips, factories, harbor facilities, highway systems, missile launching pads. For the men who dart through the atmosphere at supersonic speeds, the Iron Curtain behind which dictators like to hide is nonexistent.

Francis G. Powers will long be remembered and discussed. But, in reality, he is only a symbol of our age which has reached new frontiers. This young man from Georgia has suffered for his country. His name will be listed among the American heroes, but even he, the first American space spy of flesh and blood to be made an example of by the Russians, has been replaced by technological developments . . . two new space vehicles, the SAMOS and the MIDAS satellites.

Both of these space travelers carry cameras and infrared equipment as they orbit the earth. The pictures fall back to earth in space capsules. Their television-like equipment transmits pictures directly to earth stations.

The MIDAS is capable of giving an immediate warning of any missile launched any place on earth and of sending up a counter missile which directs and corrects itself to make a direct hit. All this in a matter of minutes.

Half a dozen such MIDAS satellites, orbiting the earth over the poles, will cover and photograph every mile of the globe on a twenty-four-hour-a-day schedule.

Pioneer Midas II, the robot spy in outer space which guards world democracy, talks to many listening posts in the free world: Kaena Point in the Hawaiian Islands, Chiniak and Kodiak in the Alaskan chain, Point Mugu and Vandenberg, California, New Boston, and Grenier, New Hampshire and Cape Canaveral, Florida.

It seems likely that this tremendous, unbelievable spy system will, in a few years, be outdated and improved, but the electronic spies of today's universe admirably demonstrate that the spies for Democracy are guardians in outer space, whirling monotonously onward to insure that no dictator on earth can ever destroy the free world from within or through surprise attacks.

Espionage seems to be eternal. Man says he does not believe in war . . . but he always speaks of war and threatens war. The Soviet Union alone controls seventeen countries since 1945. These countries were subdued through war, revolution and captured by aggression and are held by force, never through the free elective voices of the people. While men mouth statements of peace, they expend their brilliance in making bigger, better and more fantastic weapons of destruction.

The lesson these new space spies teach us today is that there is a shocking lag between our ability to build machines and our ability to solve our human problems and to iron out political difficulties. Until this gap between Twentieth Century technology and our primitive urge to fight is eliminated, we cannot hope for an everlasting peace.

Until the beginning of this century, it was considered a sort of madman's dream, like the legend of Icarus, that man could fly. He now can travel at speeds faster than sound, and scientists ponder what will happen when he reaches the speed of light. All this in less than sixty years. But the real dream of all men that we will live as nations together without conflict still remains unaccomplished.

But the day should come when our great-grandchildren will battle no more seriously than on the football fields of the moon, the Olympic tracks on Mars, the lawns of Eton and the sandlots of America . . . instead of on the bloodstained banks of the Rhine, through the bullet-ridden forests of the Argonnes, over the cold mountains of Italy or Korea.

Let us pray that the space age will prevent another war!

A POSTSCRIPT ON FRANCIS G. POWERS:

Since the publication of the first edition of this book, Powers has been tried in Moscow and sentenced to ten years of imprisonment; three in confinement and seven in a work camp. Apparently, he was a propaganda pawn in the hands of dictator Nikita Khrushchev.

Many were disappointed when Francis G. Powers did not play the role of a hero by accusing his accusers. He did not, they say, regret that he had only one life to give for his country.

Powers was never allowed to file an appeal to a higher court or to confer with a representative of the U.S. Embassy in Moscow. When his wife and parents flew to the Soviet capital, he met with them under surveillance and was not allowed to discuss his case.

Those critical of Powers point out that he carried a poison needle for suicide. He did not use it. He admitted to the Russians that he had made twenty-seven intelligence missions over the Soviet Union.

But the mystery of the Power's case has not been solved yet. Was there or was there not a tip-off about his last flight? Does his capture have any connection with Mitchell and Martin, the two code clerks who left Washington, D. C. with stolen code secrets and disappeared behind the Iron Curtain?

Name Index